Journey to the Coast

Coast FIRE, Geoarbitrage,
& Financial Independence

Copyright © 2021 One World Media, LLC
All rights reserved

This book is purely informational and represents the opinions and experiences of the author. This is not financial, tax, legal, or immigration advice. You should always seek out a qualified professional in each of these fields before making any decisions.

No part of this book may be reproduced, or stored in a retrieval system, or transmitted in any form or by any means, electronic, mechanical, photocopying, recording, or otherwise, without express written permission of the publisher.

For Isaac

It's either the hostel or the boat...

Table of Contents

Introduction

Part I - *Starting the FIRE*

For those who are new to the FIRE movement. This breaks down different approaches to FIRE, savings options, and the time value of money.

Part II - *Livin on the Road*

Using geoarbitrage after you've hit Coast FIRE and as a tool to help you get there. It covers seven potential locations for expats on FIRE.

Part III - *Ready to Hit the Coast*

For those who've achieved their savings goal and are prepared to Coast FIRE. Questions you'll want to ask yourself & practical strategies for success...

Part III – *Life on the Coast*

For those who've already Coast FIRED. Concerns you'll want to address along with what to continuously monitor.

Final Thoughts

Introduction

I hated my job. I mean I hated it so much, that the dread of going back to work after the weekend would begin just a few hours after my work week ended. I had actually hated what I was doing for a long time. A year before I quit, a friend told me, "If it's that bad, you need to just get out." Still, I had a goal – an end date and a dollar figure. I was perfectly on track. My mind kept rushing back to the early part of my career in education - living as an English teacher overseas. I can remember sleeping in my first apartment with no heat in the winter or my second apartment where I was using an outdoor bathroom with snow on the ground. I had really come so far, eighteen months of well-paid work shouldn't have been too much to handle. But it was. Luckily, my knowledge and pursuit of Coast FIRE helped me to escape a soul-destroying job and feel secure doing more of the things I love.

I had been pursuing FIRE for quite a few years. I had always known that I wanted to find a way to better balance my desire to live the life I dreamed of with my need to make a living. Stumbling onto the FIRE movement (the acronym FIRE stands for Financially Independent Retired Early) wasn't really so much an "a-ha!" moment as it was a way of syncing the goals that I already had with a well-defined path. I already knew the destination. FIRE was the map that was going to get me there. The great thing about the FIRE movement is that there are so many different paths to FIRE - some approaches have subtle differences, others stark contrasts. For me the Coast FIRE movement was the path that suited me best because it allowed me to get out of full-time work **before** reaching my full retirement number. It was also perfect for me because I love working. So, all I needed to do (after reaching my Coast FIRE number) was find a job that I love and work enough to cover my expenses (more on this below). But… I also need some security. So, I wanted to make sure that the figure I set for Coast FIRE was substantial enough to result in a portfolio balance at full retirement that would give me a financially stable and secure life.

There are, as I'll explain in the sections that follow, some risks and drawbacks to the Coast FIRE approach. So, I wanted to make sure that my path was bulletproof – or at least as close to bulletproof as possible. In this book, I'll introduce several different paths to FIRE, what Coast FIRE is and why it works for me. I'll also talk about how I've adapted this approach to fit my own needs, so I can feel as secure as possible about my financial future. Since it's such a huge part of my ability to enjoy Coast FIRE, I'll talk extensively about geoarbitrage and locations you might consider if you decide this is going to be part of how you achieve FIRE. Since I've journaled all my thoughts and experiences throughout the process of leaving my full-time work and becoming 'retired,' I'll share some of the immediate benefits that you can look forward to when you make the same switch. I'll also share the challenges that I encountered, as well as some suggestions for dealing with these challenges. I want this book to be actionable for you, so a big part of this text is composed of strategies that you can employ both as you get closer to Coast FIRE and when you do finally decide to take the plunge and leave your full-time job. In order to make this valuable to as many people as possible, I address things that early savers can try as they begin their march toward Coast FIRE, as well as practical ideas for those who are further along on the path to Coast FIRE or those who have recently hit their Coast FIRE goals.

Part I of this book is aimed at newbies. If you're just discovering the FIRE movement and are curious about what's possible, this section will get you started. For those who are already FIRE adherents, then this will serve as a review of some pertinent information. It will also expose you to some projections that will hopefully get you to see further value in Coast FIRE.

Part II is all about geoarbitrage and strategies and suggestions for getting out of dodge. Again, I want this book to have practical information that you can apply to your own life. With that in mind, I cover seven locations you should consider if you plan to move abroad. This section touches on visas available as well as the tax implications to living in some of these locations.

In Part III, I explore important questions you should ask yourself before taking the plunge into Coast FIRE. FIRE is no doubt a numbers game, but you still need to make sure that your time in Coast FIRE is as happy and fulfilling as you planned.

The fourth and final part of this book will be most important for those who've already chosen to Coast FIRE. It will ask you to periodically reevaluate your decision to leave full-time work behind and live the Coast FIRE life.

Wherever you are on this journey, I thank you for taking the time to read this book and share in my experiences. Remember that my experiences are only that – ***my*** experiences. I'm not an accountant, attorney, immigration expert, or financial advisor. This book is informational only. Always seek out the advice of an experienced financial, tax, immigration, or legal professional when making any decisions that impact your personal or financial future. If my story inspires you to ask questions about what is really possible for you and your life – then this book was worth writing.

See ya on the Coast –

Jay

PART I
Starting the FIRE

What is FIRE?

FIRE stands for Financially Independent Retired Early. It means different things to different people and there are a lot of variations of this increasingly popular movement. Simply put, it's a belief that you shouldn't have to wait until your best years are behind you to retire and start enjoying life. This belief translates into a lifestyle that is centered around planning and saving for a life where you can live off your savings and investments. Some people equate FIRE to a life of frugality (which has some truth to it), but what it is **NOT** is a life where you do without or deny yourself happiness in the name of some unspecified future goal. I live an awesome life and never find myself pinching pennies. I'm always the first guy at the table to reach for the bill. I travel more in a year than most people do in a decade, and I have an outrageously expensive coffee habit. Still, I've positioned myself to retire early and get the most out of the best years of my life. I've done this by cutting out the unnecessary expenses and channeling my income toward savings goals that have allowed me to live my best life.

The amount of money you need for your Coast FIRE figure is dependent on your full FIRE figure, so we'll discuss the latter first.

As you can see, FIRE is a numbers game. Some numbers are within your control – such as how many years until you reach full retirement or the percentage of your income that you plan to save. Some are numbers that you have less control over – such as the return on your investments and consequently, the percentage of your portfolio that you plan to withdraw in retirement. Since some of these numbers are subject to change based on market conditions and the empirical regularities of your early retirement years, there is both uncertainty and risk associated with the decision to retire early. A general rule of thumb for FIRE is that a person needs to save twenty-five times their annual expenses (not income) to reach financial independence. For example:

Total monthly expenses are $3,000 per month.

$3,000 X 12 (months) = $36,000 in annual expenses

$36,000 X 25 = $900,000

*The figure of twenty-five times annual expenses is based on the belief that you can safely withdraw 4% of your portfolio in retirement. $36,000 X 25 = $36,000 / .04 = $900,000. If you

feel that your withdrawal rate is going to be lower (or higher) you need to adjust your FIRE number accordingly. More on the 4% Rule below…

How do I get there?

Starting early is so key to retiring comfortably. Whether you're aiming for FIRE or plan to work until you're 65, starting early allows you more time to take advantage of compound returns. Let's start with a simple projection for Janet, a saver whose full retirement figure is the above mentioned $900,000. If she is able to start saving $1,500 per month, she will reach her savings goal in 23 years. This is assuming a 6% rate of return (which is reasonable). Just remember, that projections are only that – projections. Returns can vary over time, so run different projections assuming different rates of return. Let's take a look:

If Janet earned only 4% on her investments, she would have to work nearly 28 years to reach her savings goals. Conversely if she earned 8%, she would reach her goals in only 20 years. If you're just starting out, monitor your positions and how your portfolio is performing over time. Set your target allocation for your investments (between stocks and bonds) and don't forget to rebalance it every year, so as to keep the same desired allocation (more on rebalancing below). Your broker should offer some type of online dashboard with tools that let you see your performance. I use both Schwab and Fidelity, and I love the ease of use that they offer.

Our projection assumed a savings rate of $1,500 per month over the course of an entire career. It's highly unlikely that Janet would have the same savings rate throughout her entire career. Things like promotions, raises, and side jobs all have the potential to add to that person's ability to save. Homeownership, new cars, kids, and a more upscale lifestyle all eat away at money that could be filtered toward her savings goals. Above all, everyone is different, but the formulas are the same. Consider how your own situation impacts the numbers that you're going to be able to plug into those formulas.

Rebalancing

When you choose a target allocation, you are selecting the percentage of your portfolio that you want to have in different types of investments. We'll deal with stocks and bonds, though some savers choose to add other types of investments (precious metals, cryptocurrency, REITs, and more) to further diversify their portfolios. The target allocation you choose should reflect your appetite for risk as well as your need for returns. It's always best to discuss this with a financial professional who can speak to your unique situation. For our example, suppose Janet aims for a target allocation of 70% stocks and 30% bonds.

Year 1

Total Value of Investments = $100,000

Stocks = $70,000 (70% of portfolio)

Bonds = $30,000 (30% of portfolio)

After one year, Janet's investment in equities returned 12%. Her investment in bonds returned 2%. Her portfolio now looks like this:

Year 2

Total Value of Investments = $109,000

Stocks = $78,400 (72% of portfolio)

Bonds = $30,600 (28% of portfolio)

As we can see, Janet's investment allocation has changed and is no longer in line with her target allocation. She needs to sell some of those equities ($2,100) and put that into bonds. This will keep her portfolio in line with that target allocation.

Total Value of Investments = $109,000

Stocks = $76,300 (70% of portfolio)

Bonds = $32,700 (30% of portfolio)

NOTE: Always discuss the potential tax consequences of sale of assets with your tax advisor. Some accounts allow you to change an allocation without tax consequences, while others do not.

For Recent College Graduates

Such a big part of getting ahead in saving for retirement is starting early. You may have read the example of Janet in Part I and thought, "Wait! There's no way I can afford to funnel $1,500 per month toward my savings goals." While everyone's situation is different, this is a very achievable savings target – even for many new grads. In 2021, new grads were reported to earn approximately $50,000 per year as a starting salary[1]. If your employer offers a tax-advantaged retirement plan, take advantage of it. Better still, if a matching contribution is on the table, maximize this benefit. If you're earning less as a new grad (or if your appetite is to save more), consider living at home a little longer. If that's not an option, look into house hacking (renting a room in your place to a long-term roommate or on AirBnB). Making small sacrifices early can have a big impact down the road. In Part II on geoarbitrage, I'm going to cover a strategy to help new grads with no experience supercharge their path to Coast FIRE.

<u>Inflation</u>

You might be thinking, "But wait a second! Janet needs $900,000, so that she can

---

[1] https://www.cnbc.com/2021/05/13/many-college-grads-expect-to-earn-85000-in-their-first-job-this-year.html#:~:text=About%2017%25%20of%20students%20expect,most%20common%20response%20from%20students.

safely withdraw enough to cover her expenses TODAY! In twenty- or twenty-five-years' time, her expenses are not going to be the same. Aren't you forgetting about the effect of inflation?" No, the returns that I am using in these projections are real rates of return (as opposed to nominal rates of return). The real rate of return takes into account the effect of inflation. For example, if inflation is 3% and the (nominal) return on your portfolio is 9%, your real rate of return is 6%.

Real Rate of Return = Nominal Rate of Return – Inflation

NOTE: According Ian Webster at officialdata.org, the real (inflation adjusted) average annual return of the US stock market has been 6.74% since the year 1900.

How much can I withdraw when I do retire?

The 4% Rule

The 4% Rule says that you can safely withdraw 4% of your total portfolio value and never run out of money. This rule was popularized at a time when short-term interest rates were much higher than they are now. In 1994, the ten-year US Treasury

Note had a yield of roughly 7%. At the time of writing, it sits at 1.3%. In the time after the Great Recession, there were articles being written about how the 4% rule no longer holds, and that we should now consider it the 3% Rule. That is, we should consider a lower withdrawal rate in retirement so as not to run out of money. Bear in mind that your portfolio will not be entirely in bonds. It will be a mix of stocks and bonds. Your tolerance for risk will determine that allocation. Many financial advisors suggest people in retirement allocate 50% of their portfolio to stocks and 50% to bonds (a mix of corporate and treasury). If you're retiring early (and at a time with low fixed income returns), you may need to weight your portfolio more heavily toward equities. I am risk averse, so I aim for a conservative allocation that looks something more like this:

70% Stocks

30% Bonds / Cash

If you are more aggressive, you may choose to have a larger portion of your portfolio composed of stocks. Just remember the inverse relationship between risk and return. To earn the higher return that equities offer, you have to be willing to accept being exposed to more volatility. It's always good to speak to a financial professional about your retirement goals and your tolerance for risk.

While the stock market has been incredibly volatile, it has offered substantial returns since the Great Recession. The Dow bottomed out in March of 2009 at just over 6,500. At the time of writing, the Dow sits at just over 35,000. With these incredible gains, literature has emerged saying that the 4% rule is probably too conservative, and that retirees can actually afford to withdraw more in their retirement. Some have gone as far as to say that the popular belief that retirees could safely withdraw 5% in retirement (which the 4% Rule replaced) was in fact more accurate.

Following these 'professionals' over time, a simple logic prevails - when returns are strong, you can safely withdraw a larger percentage of your portfolio. When returns are less than expected, you may need to withdraw a bit less. Remember this when you're calculating your own FIRE and Coast FIRE numbers. The lower the withdrawal rate you assume, the more secure you'll be in retirement. That is, you'll be less reliant on strong returns from the market to meet your savings goals. Since you need less of your nest egg, you're less likely to run out of money. You'll also have a larger savings target for your FIRE goals. On the flip side, if you choose a higher withdrawal rate, you'll need to save less to reach your FIRE goals and thereby exit the full-time workforce sooner. You're also going to be more dependent on stronger market performance and run a higher risk of possibly running out of money in retirement.

Let's look at how this impacts your FIRE number:

For this projection, I assumed monthly expenses of $2,000.

Scenario #1:

Safe Withdrawal Rate = **5%**

Monthly Expenses: $2,000 (Annual Expenses of $24,000)

FIRE Number = $24,000 / .05 = **$480,000** (or 20 times your annual expenses)

Scenario #2:

Safe Withdrawal Rate = **4.5%**

Monthly Expenses: $2,000 (Annual Expenses of $24,000)

FIRE Number = $24,000 / .05 = **$533,333** (or 22.22 times your annual expenses)

Scenario #3:

Safe Withdrawal Rate = **4%**

Monthly Expenses: $2,000 (Annual Expenses of $24,000)

FIRE Number = $24,000 / .05 = **$600,000** (or 25 times your annual expenses)

Scenario #4:

Safe Withdrawal Rate = **3.5%**

Monthly Expenses: $2,000 (Annual Expenses of $24,000)

FIRE Number = $24,000 / .05 = **$685,714** (or 28.57 times your annual expenses)

Scenario #5:

Safe Withdrawal Rate = **3%**

Monthly Expenses: $2,000 (Annual Expenses of $24,000)

FIRE Number = $24,000 / .05 = **$800,000** (or 33.3 times your annual expenses)

You can see from the different projections above how important your safe withdrawal rate is. Our projections changed from $480,000 (at a 5% withdrawal rate) all the way up to $800,000 (at a 3% withdrawal rate)! Work out a rate that you feel most comfortable with. I run projections where I assume 3.5% to 4%. I aim for a figure in between as my full FIRE number.

Where should I save this money?

Traditional Individual Retirement Accounts (IRA)

You can open an IRA at almost any financial institution. Online brokerages make it incredibly easy to open one in a matter of minutes. For 2021, you can contribute $6,000 per year to your traditional IRA. This must be earned income – not investment income. The amount you contribute is tax deductible. It also grows tax free. However, when you withdraw the funds from your IRA, they are considered taxable income. You cannot withdraw these funds before age 59 and a half (unless you have a qualified reason for doing so), and must begin taking required minimum distributions (RMDs) by age 70 and a half. If you withdraw early, there is a 10% penalty.

Roth IRA

I absolutely love Roth IRAs! A Roth is similar to a traditional retirement account, except that you make the contributions with after-tax dollars. That means your contribution (up to $6,000 in 2021) is not tax deductible. Like a traditional IRA, the money grows tax free, AND your withdrawals in retirement are tax-free. Unlike a traditional IRA, there are income limits for a Roth. You need to earn under $140,000 in 2021 to contribute to this type of account. You can always withdraw your contributions (without tax or penalty) at any time.

Company Retirement Accounts

You should check and see if your company offers a 401k retirement account. These accounts have higher contribution limits than IRAs (up to $19,500 in 2021). Your employer may offer a matching contribution. This is the only thing better than money – it's FREE MONEY. I would suggest maxing out that matching contribution. Some companies are beginning to offer Roth 401k accounts. Which work in the same way that IRA accounts do (with after-tax contributions), but with the higher contribution limits of a 401k account. Certain types of public employees may qualify for a 403b account. Check to see what your employer provides and what the terms are.

Simplified Employee Pension (SEP IRA)

A SEP IRA is very similar to a traditional IRA in that the money deposited is pretax money and grows tax free. Any distributions that you take on your SEP are taxable as income in retirement. In most cases, you cannot withdraw from your SEP without a penalty until age 59 and a half. Like a traditional IRA, most people need to start taking RMDs from their SEP retirement account by age 70 and a half. Contributions to a SEP IRA are made by your employer. In this case- you are your employer. You are able to contribute 25% of your income (up to a maximum of $58,000 in 2021) to your own retirement. This money is a business expense, but the account belongs to the employee and grows tax free. SEP IRAs are easy to set-up and have limited reporting requirements. I was able to easily set one up with Schwab, but any online broker should be able to help you establish an account.

Savings Incentive Match Plan for Employees (SIMPLE IRA)

As a self-employed individual or an S-Corp, you can set up a SIMPLE IRA, which will allow you to contribute up to $13,500 of your salary to a tax advantaged retirement account. Much like the name implies, your employer can match your contribution (up to 3% of your salary). The contributions grow tax free until you decide to take distributions. SIMPLE IRAs have some complex rules (including those for filing and reporting), so always consult with a tax professional or a financial advisor. Some basic rules are outlined below.

- You must be a business that has less than 100 employees.

- To be eligible, an employee must have earned at least $5,000 in the two previous calendar years and be expected to earn at least $5,000 in the current calendar year.

- You must make employee contributions at the end of each month.

- You must make employer contributions at the end of each tax year.

- Employees over age 50 can contribute an extra $3,000 to catch up for their retirement.

- The employer can contribute either a flat 2% of the employee's salary or match dollar for dollar up to 3% of the employee's salary. The employer must contribute whether or not an employee contributes.

- You can begin taking distributions at age 59 and a half.

- You must begin taking required minimum distributions at age 72.

Profit Sharing Keogh

This plan functions like a 401k for the self-employed. Your contributions are tax deductible. You can contribute up $19,500 of your income as an employee in 2021. On the business side, you can match up to 25%

of that contribution – which is considered a business expense. So, these plans offer substantial tax benefits in the year that you contribute. All contributions also grow tax free. The distributions from this plan are taxed as ordinary income. The requirements to set up and maintain these plans can be a bit more cumbersome, but I was able to get assistance with someone from Fidelity. Most major online brokers should be able to assist you.

Taxable Brokerage Account

You can set up a taxable brokerage account with any one of the major online brokers. These accounts have no contribution limits, there are also no limits on when you take money out. However, contributions to these accounts are not tax advantaged. They also do not grow tax free. Any interest, dividends, or distributions would be claimed in that tax year. Depending on your tax situation, qualified dividends and long-term capital gains may be taxed at preferential rates.

When setting up any investment account, be sure to speak to a financial professional who can give you full details on how opening and investing in each account will impact your own unique financial situation.

What are some different approaches to FIRE?

Many people who retire are forced to live on less than they did during their working years. Considering that they are no longer saving for retirement (as they're already there), hopefully this doesn't restrict their lifestyle too much. My parents both lived and worked their whole lives in New York – on Long Island, where the cost of living is high. When they retired they both had social security and some small investments. The only pension was my mom's teachers' pension (which was only a percentage of her final average salary). Staying on Long Island would have really been beyond what they could afford. So, they moved to southern Georgia. They built a beautiful house in a gated community and still saw their property tax bill fall by $8,000 per year. They certainly weren't going without, but they still had to make some sacrifices. Let's face it – life in small town Georgia isn't exactly the Big Apple. They also worked full lives – both into their sixties. If your goal is FIRE, then you definitely don't want to be in the game that long. If you want to leave work earlier, but you don't want to make any sacrifices – either while you're working or in retirement, then you may want to consider Fat FIRE.

Fat FIRE

Fat Fire is the approach to FIRE that affords you the greatest flexibility and spending power in your retirement. It requires you to make fewer sacrifices while working to reach your FIRE goals. It also requires you to save the most. With Fat FIRE, your income in retirement should exceed your current expenses right now (in your working years). You don't need to move to a lower cost of living area to take advantage of geoarbitrage (more on this later). If you're located in a big city, such as New York or San Francisco, you can continue living there without working. You can maintain your same lifestyle (where you've sacrificed nothing) and also have the flexibility to travel as much as you want. To be clear, Fat FIRE is all about flexibility and security. Some people think they can leave their home in New York to move to Southeast Asia, where they can live well on $2,000 a month in retirement. This is a fantastic idea! However, I certainly don't equate this to Fat FIRE because you don't have the flexibility to move back to New York and be fully retired on $2,000 per month. You've had to sacrifice that lifestyle that you once had in New York. Fat FIRE means you can have it all! If you can save enough…

Lean FIRE

Lean FIRE requires you to tighten your belt a bit. You cut corners and make sacrifices so as to maximize your savings rate. You of course achieve this higher savings rate by cutting your monthly expenses. Since you have lower monthly expenses, this obviously reduces the number that you need to achieve your FIRE goals. *Remember that your full FIRE number is 25 times your annual expenses assuming that 4% safe withdrawal rate.* You're essentially doing double-time toward your FI figure by jacking up your savings rate and at the same time reducing the amount of your annual expenses. So, if you're a Lean FIRE adherent and willing to live on a lean budget, you can achieve FIRE much more quickly.

IMPORTANT: If Lean FIRE is how you plan to get to FI, then remember to calculate your FIRE number using the annual expenses that you would need to live the quality of life that you want in retirement. If you have roommates who split the bills with you, but you want to get rid of them once you reach FIRE, take those additional expenses into account. If you no longer want to pack your lunch every day, add the additional cost of eating out into your monthly expenses. If you're living a super restrictive lifestyle to achieve Lean FIRE, but don't want to continue to live that way once you retire, then make sure to adjust your calculations as necessary. Let's take a look at someone who needs to take this advice into account.

Jon earns $4,000 per month after taxes. He rents a room out in his house, bikes to work, and never eats out. Jon doesn't remember the last time he bought nice clothes. His total monthly expenses amount to $1,000 per month. So, Jon is able to filter $3,000 a month to his investments. Based on annual expenses of $12,000, Jon's FIRE goal is $300,000 ($12,000 X 25 = $300,000). With this savings rate and assuming a 6% real rate of return, Jon can get to his FIRE goal in less than seven years – that's incredible!

But let's face it. Jon's making some serious sacrifices to reach FI. He hates his roommate, but the guy is covering 75% of his mortgage payment (and half of the utilities). He doesn't mind cooking at home, but would like to have a bit more freedom in retirement to go out and eat. And he desperately needs a shirt that didn't come from Wal-Mart. Once he hits FIRE, he hopes to stop living such a restrictive lifestyle. With these changes, Jon's monthly expenses in retirement are going to be closer to $2,000. Let's take a look at how that changes things:

FIRE Goal = $600,000 ($24,000 X 25 = $600,000)

Monthly Savings = $3,000

Real Rate of Return on Investments = 6%

*As you can see, we haven't changed anything except Jon's FIRE goal based on his monthly expenses based on his change in lifestyle. So, let's see how this impacts time to FIRE…

Time to FIRE = approximately 140 months – or almost 12 years

Twelve years to your full FIRE number is not all that long, but just keep in mind that this is a big difference from seven years. Let's take a look at another projection for someone who has a very different situation.

Jen also earns $4,000 per month after taxes. She lives in a small house that she inherited from her parents. She has no mortgage, and her property taxes and homeowner's insurance amount to less than $200 per month. She works from home, and her hobbies mostly involve hiking, fishing, and swimming in the area around her home. She owns a used car, but rarely uses it. Without a mortgage, her monthly expenses total $1,200. Based on this, her full FIRE figure is $360,000. Jen is able to save $2,800 per *month at the same rate of 6%. Jen can reach FIRE in less than eight and a half years. Since she doesn't anticipate any change in her lifestyle, this figure is very achievable for her.*

The point is to be aware of how your expenses are going to impact your goals – and be honest with yourself about what you really need. Taking the leap into FIRE and then realizing it is unsustainable can be a huge letdown.

Barista FIRE

Barista FIRE has been popularized in the United States because of the outrageous cost of healthcare. Some people reach their savings goals and are all set to stop working when they suddenly remember that their health insurance is tied to their job. Once they quit, they have to start paying for their own health insurance. Insurance in America is nothing short of insanely expensive. The name Barista FIRE was popularized because of Starbucks' generous benefits package for their employees (partners). People who reached FIRE would work part-time at Starbucks (as a barista) to obtain the health insurance benefits. You don't need to make *triple grande nonfat one pump caramel lattes* if that's not your thing. You can seek out any part-time employment that offers health insurance. You also benefit from the additional income each month.

Another option is to search for a marketplace plan under the Affordable Care Act. Depending on your income, you may receive a credit to cover some (or even all) of the premium. Marketplace plans are nice because there are usually no pre-existing exclusions. If you're in good health, you might also choose to search for a private plan off the marketplace exchange. Bear in mind that these might have pre-existing condition exclusions or waiting periods. You can check out healthcare.gov for more information on marketplace plans. It's always good to speak to an insurance professional who can advise you on your options.

Coast FIRE

Finally! The subject of this book – Coast FIRE, allows you to take advantage of the power of compound returns to stop saving for your full FIRE number once you hit your *Coast FIRE Number*. After you've built up enough savings, you simply work to cover your monthly expenses and allow your investments to grow until they reach your full FIRE number. To calculate this *Coast FIRE*

Number, you need to plug in a few different figures.

First, you need to calculate your full FIRE number. Remember, to do this you will need to know your safe withdrawal rate.

Then you'll also need to know the number of years from when you plan to Coast FIRE (stop saving towards your retirement) until you will completely retire. This doesn't necessarily have to be your *full* retirement age (65 or 67), it is YOUR target age to stop working completely. This is important because this is the number of years that your retirement savings will grow through the power of compounding. The longer that your portfolio has to grow, the less you will need to reach your FIRE figure (and the sooner you can Coast FIRE). Just think – if you put $100,000 away for twenty-five years at 6% per annum, you're going to have more money than if you put it away for ten years at that same 6%.

Also, you need to decide what rate of return you're going to give yourself. If you're a bit more conservative, you'll want to choose a lower rate of return. If you're confident that your investments will return more, you can project out using that higher rate of return. I prefer to be a bit more conservative in my planning and (hopefully) be pleasantly surprised when it's time for full retirement. Let's take a look at some projections:

Assume that Eric's total expenses are $3,000 per month and he doesn't expect to have any major lifestyle changes in retirement the way Jon did. Eric anticipates being able to have a safe withdrawal rate of 4% of his total portfolio. So, his full FIRE number is $900,000. He projects a 6% real rate of return on his investments, and wants to Coast FIRE at age 45 before fully retiring at age 65 (so his investments will have twenty years to grow via the magic of compound returns. His formula for computing his Coast FIRE number looks like this:

Full FIRE Number / (1 + Expected Rate of Return) ^ # Years from Coast FIRE to Full Retirement

900,000 / (1 + 0.06) ^ 20 = $249,754

NOTE: You can easily complete this calculation on your phone's calculator by typing: 900,000 / 1.06 x^2

Your screen should look like this: 900,000 ÷ 1.06 ^ (2)

Simply move the cursor over to the (2) and change it to (20). Your final formula should look like this:

900,000 ÷ 1.06 ^ (20) = $249,754

This means that Eric only has to save $249,754 by age 45 to be ready to coast into retirement. Eric is still going to need to work to cover his monthly living expenses, but he should be able to completely stop making retirement savings contributions.

As you can see, this is incredibly achievable! Even if Eric saves nothing throughout his twenties, this is still well within his reach. He can begin saving on his 30th birthday and earns 6% per annum on his investments, he'll only need to save $871 per month to reach his Coast FIRE number. Just remember, there are so many moving parts in the FIRE and Coast FIRE calculations. As you read through this book and look at the different projections and scenarios, think about how you can adjust your lifestyle so as to align your spending and savings rates to reach your goals as fast as possible. One of the numbers that has the largest impact and is well within your control is your annual expenses. If you can lower this figure, you can fast track your way to Coast FIRE.

Perhaps one of the easiest ways to do this is by taking advantage of geoarbitrage.

PART II
Livin on the Road

What is geoarbitrage?

Geoarbitrage involves moving to an area with a lower cost of living – either within your home country or abroad, while maintaining a standard of income consistent with what you're earning at home. Taking advantage of the lower cost of living allows you to significantly lower your annual expenses, and consequently lowering your FIRE and Coast FIRE numbers. Many Americans are making the choice to retire to overseas locations. Places like Portugal, Spain, Bali, Costa Rica, Ecuador, Mexico, or Belize offer incredible lifestyles and far lower living costs. And these are only a few of the places that retirees are flocking to. A $450,000 portfolio is probably not going to be sufficient for full FIRE in most parts of the USA. This portfolio would only allow you to withdraw $1,500 per month (assuming a 4% safe withdrawal rate), but this could be enough to get by in many of the countries listed above. Many older retirees who have little or no savings are forced to rely on social security. As a result, they have chosen locations abroad as a way to make their income in retirement go further. Taking advantage of geoarbitrage is not only a great strategy for those who are fully retired – whether it's a traditional retirement age or early retirement, but it can also have the effect of dramatically shortening your time to Coast FIRE.

For those who are locked into great jobs that require them to physically be in the USA and are well on their way to Coast FIRE, it may make little sense to leave. But if you're not getting to your Coast FIRE goals as quickly as you'd like…. WHY WAIT? Take advantage of all the remote work opportunities to combine geoarbitrage with your journey to FIRE.

As I mentioned, certain approaches to FIRE can involve some degree of frugality. Stop for a moment and ask yourself, "What expenses can I dramatically cut in my life right now?" If you're like most folks, your answers probably center on discretionary expenses, such as entertainment, eating out, or buying new clothes. What you probably DON'T include are things like- housing, electricity & running water, health insurance, or groceries. However, if you're living in the United States or Canada, it's these non-discretionary expenses that eat up the biggest portion of your budget. Or, as a FIRE adherent, represent money that is NOT being funneled toward your savings and investment.

Choosing to live in another country with a much lower cost of living allows you to dramatically cut these expenses and dedicate a larger portion of your income toward your savings goals. What's more? You may get to do all of this by working a schedule that's far less demanding than what you'd find at home in America (or many other Western countries). So, in many respects, you're semi-retired while planning for your early retirement. Let's look at some ways that geoarbitrage can help you more quickly get to your Coast FIRE goals..

The High Cost of Living in America

Rent & Utilities

Let's face it, this likely makes up the biggest portion of our monthly budget. In America (and most other Western countries), it ain't cheap to live! The average monthly rent in the US stands at approximately $1,400 per month. Now, America is a big place, and the cost of living varies dramatically depending on where you choose to live. However, most folks who aren't living in a shoebox in the middle of nowhere will find that figure fairly accurate. When my parents retired and moved out of New York, they moved to a very small country town in rural Georgia (about as close to the middle of nowhere as possible). Even there, the average rent on a one-bedroom apartment is $700. A two-bedroom apartment in the same small town costs $875.

Now the exciting part begins- adding in all of your monthly bills. I am going to use my most recent bills in rural Georgia as a guide.

Cable, Telephone, & Internet- $130

Water- $60

Electricity- $150 (average)

Cell Phone- $50

You'll notice that I've only included your basic utilities. If you rent a home, add $15 per month for renter's insurance. If you OWN your home, you need to add expenses for homeowner's insurance, flood insurance, homeowner's association or condo fees, and property taxes. I didn't include lawn care on this list. If you don't live in an apartment or a condo where this is taken care of for you, you can do it yourself or you can add approximately $175 per month.

Again, it's important to consider **WHERE** you live. These projections should serve as a guide to get you thinking about your own situation, inserting figures that apply to your own living circumstances, and seeing how geoarbitrage can make an impact on your Coast FIRE goals. I have a friend in New York who pays over $300 for cable, phone, and internet. So, as you can see, costs vary wildly depending on your location.

Let's ballpark my example from above. Total monthly living costs should cost you- $1105/per month to rent the shoebox in Georgia, or up to $1805 if you go with the average cost of rent in the US. For the purposes of this projection, let's meet in the middle and call it **$1455 per month** for your rent and bills in the US. I am SURE this is on the low side for most in the US – and we didn't even touch on transportation. Car payments, insurance, and maintenance aren't cheap! Now let's look at how those taking advantage of geoarbitrage can dramatically cut their expenses.

Do you work remotely? The world is your oyster! All you need is some high-speed Wi-Fi!

Let's look at a spot in southeast Asia that no one would complain about being stuck in - **Bali, Indonesia**. In Bali, the rent can vary wildly, but I'll use figures from my own experience:

Studio apartment (w/ swimming pool): 2.6 million rupiah (or about $180 USD/month)

Electricity: Approximately $20

High Speed Internet: $50

Cable TV: Included

Water: Included

Cell Phone: $20

This brings your total monthly living expenses to $270 USD- a savings of nearly $1,200!!!

Before you say it…. "*Sure, that's just one spot!"* Yes, this represents one of an infinite number of possibilities for remote workers, but you'll find comparable opportunities for living in places all over Southeast Asia.

Yeah, but you EARN more in the US!

The Covid-19 pandemic has changed so much in all of our lives. One of the bright spots to come out of this horrible time is that employers are now far more open to remote work. Globally distributed work teams are growing in popularity. Thereby making it likely that you could earn the same salary in the exact same job you're doing now while taking advantage of geoarbitrage to lower your cost of living. If your boss is opposed to it, then suggest a 'test run' of one or two days a week. Also bear in mind that employers may be far more open to allowing workers to stay on remotely if they think the alternative is losing someone who is highly valued. If this is the path you really want to take, don't be afraid to walk away. Just remember that if you play that card, you have to be willing to accept the reality that your boss may let you go. Honestly gauge your worth to the company and the job's value in your own life. If all else fails, you might choose to offer to work in a remote role at a reduced salary. Do the math and see if the difference in salary is more than offset by the lower cost of living. If you come out ahead, you might be willing to take the lower pay. Average salaries vary by state. In a place like New York City, the average individual salary is $75,000 per year (according to the US Census Bureau). Bear in mind, that you are NOT going to live in New York City for the above mentioned $1,455 a month inclusive of all monthly bills. Figures will be MUCH higher. In states where it is less expensive to live, the average salaries tend to be lower- some as low as $40k (think Mississippi). Taking advantage of geoarbitrage allows you to dramatically cut your expenses, and in many cases work much less. Thereby enjoying a vastly improved quality of life.

Health Insurance:

As we've already established, healthcare in the USA is insanely expensive. Many Americans have full-time jobs with good health insurance. Well-deserved! Just remember, once you Coast FIRE, that insurance may disappear with your full-time work schedule. If not, you are faced with private options or the Affordable Care Act. If you have pre-existing conditions, you almost certainly need a policy from the ACA. In 2018, I paid over $600 per month for poor coverage. In 2019, I was paying $400- again with limited options. Living abroad, you can get private, global coverage based on your age. BUPA, a British company, offers reasonable rates for global coverage (excluding the USA). Cigna Global is another option that is popular with Americans living abroad. Of course, the younger you are, the cheaper your coverage.

As a 40-year-old, I received a BUPA quote of around $200USD/month for excellent coverage. World Nomads offered me great travel insurance for about $100 a month.

Cheaper still, is if you can get into the public/private system where you are basing yourself. In Portugal, it is possible to get private health insurance with very reasonable levels of coverage for less than 50 euros per month! It's tough to come up with an exact figure that you'll save on health insurance, but it's hard to imagine health care being **MORE** expensive outside of America.

Entertainment

Did I mention America is an expensive place to live? Try going out for dinner and drinks with your significant other and walking away with change from $100. There are many FIRE adherents in the US who manage to enjoy themselves without unnecessary expenditures on eating out, but it can be tough. It can be socially isolating too because you may find yourself constantly turning down invitations to go out for dinner or head to a local bar to have a drink. Living overseas changes all of that. Sure, there are expensive options, but you can get dinner for two and a few drinks at a small restaurant in Bali for less than $15. There are options here in Europe that are comparable- less than 20 Euros for dinner and a few drinks. Now, there certainly ARE more expensive options. Just remember that you can still enjoy the benefits of going out without breaking the bank. The money you're saving is fueling your early retirement. If you feel paying $10 for a cocktail with a fancy umbrella in it is worth it, then have it- just remember the opportunity cost that goes with it. For me, I'd much rather grab a beer from a local convenience store for $1.50 and sit on the beach with a few friends.

Grocery Shopping:

Again, this is something that is specific to the person and their own lifestyle. America is expensive to live. *Have I mentioned that?* In Portugal, milk, bread, chicken, and fruits & veggies are all reasonably priced. The same is true in many parts of southeast Asia. Figures that I've seen online indicate an average grocery bill of $250 USD per month for a person living in America. This seems low for what food costs at home (particularly for fresh fruits and vegetables). Still, food shopping in many locations overseas should put less of a strain on your budget.

Transport:

If you have a car in the US, insurance and car payments can be a killer. They can really eat up your budget. If you're brave enough to get on a motorbike in southeast Asia, this expense can drop to $50 per month. Car insurance, taxes, and payments can vary depending on where you are in the world. Consider your public transport options and make a decision that best suits your FIRE goals.

There are two different strategies those in pursuit of coast fire can employ to take advantage of geoarbitrage – waiting until you FIRE to move abroad OR moving overseas immediately to help reduce your time to Coast FIRE.

#1 –First achieving your Coast FIRE number in your home country, and THEN taking advantage of geoarbitrage to live more cheaply in retirement

#2 – Moving to a lower cost of living location as a remote worker to take advantage of the lower cost of living and the higher savings rate to achieve Coast FIRE more quickly

Let's look at the first option.

#1 – Hitting Coast FIRE at Home and _Then_ Moving to a LCOL Country:

Your Coast FIRE number is set based on the expenses you plan to have in the low-cost of living country. However, by taking this route to Coast FIRE, you get to earn that relatively larger American salary. However, you also have those relatively larger American expenses. This approach might be right for you if one or more of the following apply to you:

· You are in a well-paid position at home.

· Working remotely is simply not an option for you.

· Your savings rate is substantial enough to allow you to hit your Coast FIRE target within a decade.

· Your American employer provides you with health insurance.

· You still have children / family that are keeping you in the States for the time being.

· Leaving the position that you're in would make it very difficult to return to a similar role.

If you have a great job at home (and it isn't driving you to the nuthouse), then it might be worth staying on with your current employer. The cost of living in America is relatively high, but so are the salaries. This is particularly true for people who are mid-career and at that peak earnings point. I outlined some approaches you may choose to take with your boss to see if remote work is an option for you, but if it's not, then it might be worth hanging on. This is especially true if you're in a competitive position for which there aren't many openings. If walking away would make it impossible to come back, then definitely think long and hard before going.

All of this is complicated by the fact that many top positions have health insurance benefits tied to them. Leaving that position would require you to cover your own health insurance premiums or run for the border. I would personally choose to run for the border before I paid for my own health insurance in America. But just remember – once you leave that job, you're no longer tied to America. You now have the option to leave the country and take advantage of significantly more affordable healthcare abroad. But if you want to stay at home a bit longer or if you have kids whom you want to finish school, you may want to hold on to those health insurance benefits. Many parents prefer to have their kids finish school at home before moving abroad in pursuit of their FIRE goals. That's a personal choice that's specific to your situation, though I have seen many families that live abroad with their kids. Raising kids in another country may even be advantageous for them in terms of safety, quality of education, and personal growth.

For all the anxiety that people have about quitting their jobs too soon, it is probably easier than you might think to get that job back (or a similar one). Don't put your dreams off forever. If you can't reach Coast FIRE in your well-paid American job within ten years, then think about jumping ship. If it doesn't work out, there's nothing stopping you from going back to your old life. In the next section I'm going to outline some paths for achieving Coast FIRE *while* taking advantage of geoarbitrage at the same time. As you'll see, it's not always about how much you make, but how much you keep. Moving abroad might just make it *easier* to reach your Coast FIRE goals.

#2 – Moving to a LCOL Location <u>*WHILE*</u> Working to Achieve Coast FIRE:

Lowering your annual expenses in retirement is going to give you those lower FIRE and Coast FIRE numbers. As the section above outlined, geoarbitrage is a great way to dramatically reduce your living expenses in retirement. Reducing your expenses while you're still working in pursuit of Coast FIRE can also boost your savings rate to the point that you are able to actually achieve Coast FIRE more quickly than if you'd remained in the USA. This approach might be right for you if one or more of the following apply to you:

- You have a well-paid job that allows you to engage in location-independent work.

- Your current job at home doesn't allow you to save anything.

    o Your salary is incredibly low.

    o You live in a high cost of living (HCOL) area.

- You're sick of your career (even if it is well-paid) and desperate for a change.

- You have the skills to harness technology for location-independent work.

    o You are an entrepreneur.

    o You can learn and utilize the skills necessary to take advantage of remote work opportunities.

- You have nothing tying you to your home country.

    o You're single or have a partner with a similar mindset.

    o You have no kids or family members that depend on you.

- You adapt easily to other countries and cultures.

- You have a sense of adventure.

For those people who are able to maintain a well-paid job in the USA and live in a country with a low-cost of living, the time to Coast FIRE can be just a few short years. If you can earn $100,000 USD per year and live off of $1,500 per month, you can sock away a very large portion of your salary. Let's take a look at a very financially conservative 35-year-old lady who earns $100,000 per year:

Salina is 35 and wants to Coast FIRE by age 40 and fully retire by age 60.

Gross Salary: $100,000

After-Tax Salary: $77,247*

Monthly Salary: $6,437.25

Monthly Expenses: $1,500

Total Monthly Savings: $4,937.25

FIRE NUMBER = $800,000 (This is based on $24,000 in annual expenses and a 3% safe withdrawal rate)

Coast FIRE Number: $301,511 (This is based on a 5% annualized real return over her 20 years of Coast FIRE – age 40 to 60.)

If Salina has NOTHING saved, and earns a 5% real return on her investment, she can reach her goal in less than 55 months (about four and half years).

This is an incredibly conservative estimate. Her current expenses are only $1,500 per month, yet she assumed $2,000 a month for her calculation (giving her a bit of breathing room). She also assumed a safe withdrawal rate of 3% (instead of the more traditional 4%). Finally, she assumed her investments would earn an after-tax return of only 5%. She still got there in less than five years! You may have noticed an asterisk by her after-tax salary. That is because for this calculation, we assumed that she still pays US federal income taxes. This calculation only used her standard deduction as a single filer. It didn't include any deductions for tax-advantaged savings accounts (such an IRA or 401k). It also didn't include the possibility of her being able to take advantage of the Foreign Earned Income Exclusion (FEIE).

For our next projection, let's assume that she has the same tax liability. Only this time, we're going to calculate her FIRE number using her actual expenses of $1,500 per month, assume a more traditional withdrawal rate of 4, and give her a 6% real rate of return on her investments.

Gross Salary: $100,000

After-Tax Salary: $77,247*

Monthly Salary: $6,437.25

Monthly Expenses: $1,500

Total Monthly Savings: $4,937.25

FIRE NUMBER = $450,000 (This is based on $18,000 in annual expenses and a 4% safe withdrawal rate)

Coast FIRE Number: $140,312 (This is based on a 6% annualized real return over her 20 years of Coast FIRE – age 40 to 60.)

What an incredible difference! Salina's Coast FIRE number just fell by over $160,000! With her rate of savings, she can reach this figure in less than 27 months! Just over two years!

If Salina qualifies for the FEIE, she could wind up with a take home salary of $92,350 per year (or $7,695 per month). This would boost her monthly savings to $6,195! It would also shorten her time to Coast FIRE to just under 22 months – less than two years! Salina could hit her coast FIRE goal by age 37. That means she would actually have more time to let her nest egg grow! So, she would need less. Her Coast FIRE number 37 would only be $117,000 because it now has 23 years to grow (instead of 20). So, Selina could Coast FIRE a bit earlier (or simply enjoy the extra cushion). As these projections show, you can reach Coast FIRE incredibly quickly by earning a top American salary and taking advantage of geoarbitrage.

Salina was able to do it in less than two years! That's not fantasy – it's just math.

Always be aware of the taxation requirements of the country that you choose to call home, and always consult a tax professional who can advise you of your tax liabilities (both in the USA and in your new home country). Many countries offer enticing tax incentives for foreigners to come and move there (remember Portugal and Ecuador are two such countries). Check and see how these potentially money-saving tax incentives apply to you.

What if I don't earn $100,000 a year?

Moving Abroad with a More Modest Income

Let's take a look at how you can live and save by taking advantage of geoarbitrage even if you don't earn a top US salary. Due to Covid, more companies than ever are outsourcing jobs to remote workers. For this next projection, we are going to look at Tom, who earns a modest salary as a freelance executive assistant. I assumed an income of $2,000 per month, and self-employment and income taxes for a single filer. I'm using the same figures for living expenses as the person living in Bali, Indonesia.

Income After Tax: $1800

Expenses:

Rent & Utilities: $270

Transport: $80

Groceries: $150

Entertainment (eating out): $300

Travel Insurance: $100

Total Expenses = $900

Disposable Income available for Investment in Your Early Retirement = $900 / month

Again, this is assuming a very modest online income. There is a lot of remote work available at the moment. The more you take on, the more disposable income you will have to devote to your early retirement. Just make sure you don't do it at the expense of your current life.

So, let's see how geoarbitrage and the magic of compounding- earnings on earnings, can help Tom reach his Coast FIRE goals.

First, we need to compute his full FIRE number. Current annual expenses are $10,800 ($900 / month). Let's give Tom some cushion and assume annual expenses of $12,000 ($1,000 / month). Assuming a 4% safe withdrawal rate, Tom's full FIRE number is $300,000.

Following the schedule above and saving $900 per month with a goal of a $300,000 nest egg.

This should allow a $1,000 a month withdrawal from savings without ever running out of money.

Assuming a 6% average annual rate of return

Let's look at different projections assuming different levels of savings.

No Savings

Saving $900 per month, Tom would have $300,000 in savings in about **16 & a half years**.

$10,000 Savings

Saving $900 per month, Tom would have $300,000 in savings in about **15 & a half years**.

$20,000 Savings

Saving $900 per month, Tom would have $300,000 in savings in about **14 years & 9 months**.

$50,000 Savings

Saving $900 per month, Tom would have $300,000 in savings in about **12 years & 5 months**.

$100,000 Savings

Saving $900 per month, Tom would have $300,000 in savings in about **9 years & 1 month**.

Let's repeat the following scenarios with a higher savings rate- $1,500 per month

No Savings

Saving $1500 per month, Tom would have $300,000 in savings in about **11 years & eight months**.

$10,000 Savings

Saving $1500 per month, Tom would have $300,000 in savings in about **11 years & 1 month**.

$20,000 Savings

Saving $1500 per month, Tom would have $300,000 in savings in about **10 years & 7 months**.

$50,000 Savings

Saving $1500 per month, Tom would have $300,000 in savings in about **9 years and 1 month**.

$100,000 Savings

Saving $1500 per month, Tom would have $300,000 in savings in about **6 years and 10 months**.

NOTE: These are for <u>full FIRE numbers</u>.

Let's look at <u>Coast FIRE</u> projections for Tom. We are going to assume that he is moving abroad at age 35 and plans to fully retire at age 60. We'll assume a 6% rate of return. Remember our formula:

Full FIRE Number / (1 + Expected Rate of Return) ^ # Years from Coast FIRE to Full Retirement

With no savings, Tom would be able to Coast FIRE in ten years (at age 45) by saving $900 per month.

$300,000 / 1.06 ^ 15 = **$125,180**

Tom would actually have a bit more than the necessary $125,180. The total savings after ten years would be **$146,227**.

Let's repeat the same projection assuming that higher savings rate of $1,500 per month.

With no savings, Tom would be able to Coast FIRE in five years (at age 40) by saving $1,500 per month.

$300,000 / 1.06 ^ 20 = **$93,541**

Tom would actually have a bit more than the necessary $93,541. The total savings after ten years would be **$104,230**.

The purpose of these projections is to get you to see the time value of money and get you thinking about early retirement and how geoarbitrage can help to make it possible. Early retirement will give you the freedom to make choices based on what you *WANT* to do, as opposed to what you *NEED* to do.

Where can I go?

Locations to Take Advantage of Geoarbitrage

There are a lot of fantastic locations where you can live for a fraction of what it costs to live in the USA. Some fantastic options include Portugal, Spain, Ecuador, Bali, Costa Rica, Mexico, and Belize.

Portugal

Portugal makes the top of this list for several reasons. It's incredibly affordable to live. The average salary in Portugal is less than 10,000 euros per year. Real estate outside the big cities is ridiculously cheap to either rent or own. Portugal offers universal healthcare to residents. While the public system is not without hiccups, the private healthcare is exceptional and very affordable. What makes Portugal such an attractive option is ten years of tax-preferred treatment. Under Portugal's non-habitual residency scheme, certain types of income (such as pension, dividends, and interest) is taxed at a preferential rate of 10%. After five years, you can apply for citizenship, which brings the benefit of an EU passport. It's important to note that after ten years, you are required to pay the same rates as a Portuguese tax resident – and tax rates are very high here.

For more details on immigrating to Portugal (including visas and tax benefits), check out one of my other Kindle publications: *Move to Portugal*

Spain

Portugal's neighbor is another incredible option for early retirement. The lifestyle is incredible. While big cities like Madrid and Barcelona can be pricey, smaller towns and cities offer very affordable living options. Spanish public healthcare is excellent. Those who wish to supplement public care with private insurance will find it very affordable. Spain does offer a pathway to citizenship and an EU passport. However, it's a longer process than Portugal's. Spain doesn't offer any preferential tax treatment either – and the taxes are high. Many retirees opt for the non-lucrative visa, which requires you to spend 183 days per year in Spain (thereby making you a resident for tax purposes).

Ecuador

Ecuador offers cheap and easy visa options for foreigners wishing to retire there. Temporary visas are valid for one year and can be renewed once. After 21 months, you are able to apply for permanent residency. After three years living as a permanent resident, you can apply for Ecuadorian citizenship. Temporary visas can be obtained through investment of approximately $40,000 – (either by purchasing a property or by making a deposit into an approved Ecuadorian bank), or by meeting certain educational requirements. Ecuador has adequate and affordable private healthcare. It also offers a diversity of living options – from mountains to beaches. So long as your income is sourced from the USA, you are only taxed in the USA - which makes things incredibly convenient.

Bali, Indonesia

Bali is on my list as it is so beautiful and so cheap to live. I believe that it has the cheapest living options of any place on this list – so long as you are willing to sacrifice a little. Luxury villas in Bali are NOT cheap. In fact, they're expensive – even by American standards. If you are willing to get a small studio apartment (called a *kos*), you can live for next to nothing. For about $100 per month, you can find a clean, comfortable *kos*. There are cheaper options available, but they may not meet an acceptable standard. If you are not old enough for a retirement visa, you will have to jump through some hoops to get a social visa. This visa is valid for six months in total. It is granted for a period of 60 days and is extendable for four additional periods of 30 days. It requires a trip to immigration and about $25 to extend it. On the downside, the medical care in Bali is awful. I would strongly suggest having international health cover that includes evacuation insurance. In the event of any medical emergency, it's always best to fly to a location with more advanced healthcare options, such as Singapore, Kuala Lumpur, or Bangkok.

Costa Rica

I first traveled to Costa Rica twenty-five years ago. I traveled down dirt roads lined with tiny food stalls and stopped in lots of idyllic small towns along the way. I've been back several times since then. Those roads have all been paved, supermarkets have been built, and luxury villas aimed at expat retirees are going up everywhere. Costa Rica certainly isn't the bargain that it once was, but it's still a beautiful country with amazing people and relatively affordable when compared to the USA. The capital city of San Jose offers fantastic healthcare, and visas are not difficult to obtain. The retirement visa has no minimum age and requires income of $1,000 per month. However, this needs to come from a pension or an annuity – and be guaranteed for life. The requirement drops to $750 if you purchase a home for $100,000 in Costa Rica. For those without private pensions, you may qualify for a *rentista* visa which requires a monthly income of $2,500 guaranteed for at least two years.

Belize

A Central American paradise with Caribbean vibes? Yes, please! Belize is becoming increasingly popular with expats. In addition to its natural beauty, it's very cheap to live. Belize also offers several different types of residency visas. If you are an American or EU citizen, you do not require a visa for stays up to 30 days. This initial 30-day visa can be renewed for up to six months. Retirees with a monthly pension of at least $1,000 can qualify for a visa. If you are not retired, but have passive income from other sources, you can still qualify (though the requirement increases to $2,000 per month). If you are self-employed or want to build your side hustle under the shade of a palm tree, then the business/visitor visa may be an option for entrepreneurs.

Mexico

I have friends who chose to retire early to Mexico, and I don't blame them one bit! Having spent considerable time there, I could see how anyone would want to call that country home. Another huge advantage of living in Mexico is your ability to be in close proximity to family and friends in the USA. If you want to live abroad, but you don't want to deal with the twenty-five hours of travel from Bali to America, then Mexico is a great option. You can qualify for a visa with pension income of less than $2,000. If your income is not from a pension, you can still qualify with investment income in the same amount AND savings of approximately $30,000. After four years, you can apply for permanent residency.

What about Social Security?

We've been talking exclusively about private savings to fund your retirement. One thing that we haven't addressed is government pensions, such as social security. Part of the path to Coast FIRE is to work enough to cover your expenses until you reach full-retirement age. Once you hit your full retirement age, the magic of compounding (and the regular monitoring of your investments) should have helped your portfolio to reach the figure that you had envisaged for your full retirement. At which point, you'll begin taking distributions to cover your expenses. If you adhere to your safe withdrawal rate (I'm using the 4% rule), you should be able to cover your expenses for life. Remember – this assumes no other income in retirement. But if you've earned enough credits to qualify, you may receive Social Security payments to offset your living costs during your full retirement. This additional monthly income in your retirement may cover some or all of your retirement expenses. Before we look at how Social Security can impact your path to Coast

FIRE, let's build some background on the topic.

Will I qualify for Social Security?

It depends. To qualify for retirement benefits, you need to have accumulated 40 Social Security credits. You can earn up to four credits per year for full or part-time work. So, you need ten years of work to qualify for some retirement benefits. In 2021, you need to earn $1,470 to get one Social Security credit. Once you earn $5,880, you will have earned the maximum of four credits for that year. You can check your number of credits and what your future benefit may look like on the Social Security Administration (SSA) website. I consider my Social Security to be an investment. Just as I monitor my portfolio of stocks, bonds, and alternative assets, I also monitor my Social Security. If you don't already have an account at ssa.gov that you regularly check, I would encourage you to do so.

How much will I get?

How much you get in a retirement benefit will depend on how much you have made over the course of your lifetime. Your **highest 35 years of earnings** are indexed for wage growth and then averaged. The

SSA uses this to calculate your benefit. It's important to note that if you work less than 35 years, then the SSA adds zeros into the calculation of your average earnings. For example, if you had average earnings of $45,000 over 25 years of employment, the SSA would divide your total earnings by 35 years. This would bring your average salary down from $45,000 to $32,142. The calculation would be performed as follows:

($45,000 X 25 years) = $1,125,000 / 35 = $32,142

Continuing to work on the road to Coast FIRE, even if your earnings are not especially substantial, can help to eliminate any zeros that might be averaged into your final average wage, and thus your benefit calculation. Remember only Social Security wages are included in this calculation. Other types of income (rents, dividends, interest, or capital gains) are not exposed to Social Security tax and thus don't impact your benefit.

What if I am self-employed?

If you are self-employed, you are still responsible for paying your payroll taxes (both the employer and employee portion). Unfortunately, you don't get double the credits! If you are a sole proprietor (and filing a Schedule C with your federal tax return), your net income is the amount that you would pay Social Security and Medicare tax on. This would also be the number that the SSA adds to your average wage calculation for your 35 years of earnings. If your business is organized as an S-Corp or an LLC that is taxed as an S-Corp, you are a separate legal entity from the business. However, you still need to pay yourself a reasonable wage for the work that you perform. This wage that you pay yourself, which you would receive on a form W-2, is the amount that you would pay Social Security and Medicare tax on. This would also be the number that the SSA adds to your average wage calculation for your 35 years of earnings. It is important to note here that the income from the business side is not exposed to Social Security and Medicare taxes. So, you can enjoy an immediate savings in payroll taxes. However, the wage that the SSA adds to your average wage calculation would be lower (potentially resulting in a lower benefit). Let's take a look at two examples – one for a self-employed individual who operates as a sole proprietor and another for someone who organizes her business as an S-Corp.

Type of Entity	Sole Proprietor	S-Corporation
Total Revenue	$60,000	$60,000
Business Expenses	$10,000	$10,000
Salary Expense (paid to self)	$0	$30,000
Business Income	$50,000	$20,000

In this case, the sole proprietor has to pay Social Security and Medicare taxes on $50,000 and would have this figure used in their average wage calculation. The owner of the S-Corp would only have to pay Social Security and Medicare taxes on $30,000 would have this lower figure used in their average wage calculation.

I firmly believe that it's so important to pay into social security. First, it's the law and going to jail would suck. Second, it provides you another source of income in retirement – one that is indexed for inflation and not exposed to sequence of returns risk. It adds stability to your Coast FIRE experience.

NOTE: Everyone's tax situation is unique. Please be sure to consult a certified tax professional in your home country and your home abroad to ensure that you are complying with all tax laws.

Can I still get SSA if I take advantage of geoarbitrage and live abroad?

Yes! The US government does have a few restrictions as to where they send money too, but the list is short. As long as your retirement plans don't include a beach house in North Korea, you should be cool. My mother is retired in Portugal and receives her social security checks via direct deposit to her US bank account.

What changes are coming?

No one knows for sure. A common question that people ask is, "Is Social Security going to be broke by the time that I retire?" That is a very valid question. Social Security is a "pay as you go" system, which means that current payroll tax payments are used to cover current payments to retirees. There is a Social Security trust fund. However, this is being depleted at a rapid pace. It's going to be up to lawmakers to act to save Social Security. The question is – "Will they?" Social Security remains one of the most popular federal programs, so I doubt that self-interested politicians are going to let it die. Even if they didn't act to save the program (so as to ensure you would be paid your full retirement benefit), the trust fund is projected to be able to pay full benefits until the year 2034, after which time the current payroll tax contributions would still be able to cover approximately 76% of scheduled benefits. This is based on the 2020 report from the Social Security Administration, *Status of the Social Security and Medicare Programs*.

The reason that this book didn't touch on Social Security in Part I, and why I don't include Social Security in my FIRE calculation, is because there is so much uncertainty surrounding it. Policy briefs from the Social Security Administration (which can be found at ssa.gov) show that efforts to save the program, or increased payroll taxes, have been explored for some time now. I honestly believe that my full retirement benefits will be there to help me cover my expenses when I completely retire. However, I want to be confident that I can retire even if Social Security were to disappear completely – if I get anything from Social Security it is going to be a bonus.

It's not all bad news!

With all the focus on whether your Social Security check will be less than what you expected, some people may find that their check may actually be more than what they expected. While campaigning for President, Joe Biden suggested that he would support an increase in the minimum Social Security benefit based on the federal poverty level. Again, this is by no means a certainty. Without an increase in benefits, Social Security won't be able to cover what they owe Americans in 2034. So, I wouldn't bank on that extra cash until it's in your account. So, like I said – if I get a benefit check, it's a bonus! If not, I want to have a plan in place to be sure I can cover my expenses.

If I Was a Recent College Graduate...

Starting Young

While there may be differences – some subtle and some stark, as to how people reach FIRE, there is one thing you will hear over and over – START EARLY. The earlier you start, the longer your money has to grow. Remember that the more years you spend in Coast FIRE before full retirement, the longer your money has to grow through compound returns. As the projections above indicated, geoarbitrage is attractive regardless of your level of income. In fact, it may be the best opportunity to achieve FIRE for those people who are in low-paid jobs or whose salary just covers their living expenses. If this sounds a lot like recent college graduates, that's probably because it is. Earlier, it was noted that the average starting salary is approximately $50,000. If you're earning this salary, I'd encourage you to do what's necessary to aim for that higher savings rate (at least $1,500). If you're an engineer or working in IT, you may have the opportunity to save even more right out of college. However, as a 22-year-old, all recent grads have something on their side that many other people on the path to Coast FIRE don't have and can never get back – TIME. You have more time to let your savings grow. One job that allows you to take advantage of geoarbitrage, save money, and requires little to no experience is teaching English abroad. It is an excellent and easily accessible path to Coast FIRE. One where you can achieve your goals in as little as five years.

There are a lot of people who choose to live and teach abroad because they want to escape responsibility at home. They party it up and many wind up saving nothing. A lot of these same people will tell you that achieving financial independence teaching English is entirely impossible. Remember – FIRE is just numbers. If the math adds up, then it adds up. If those people want to indulge in a lifestyle that suits them, then more power to 'em. If they want to tear you down for trying to reach your goals, then screw 'em. Trust me when I say that achieving FIRE while teaching abroad is entirely possible. I know because I did it. I only wish that I would have started earlier.

First of all, not all jobs teaching abroad are created equal. There are a lot of awesome locations where you can go live, teach, make enough to get by, and have an unforgettable experience. I did that for a year in Bali (earning $800 a month). I spent a year living the dream and was able to get by on what I made. I saved nothing, but I had a great time. That's not what we're aiming for here. We want to find a job that's going to let us save as much of our salary as possible. For recent graduates with a degree in education, consider searching for international school jobs. Many offer exceptional salaries, benefits, and include accommodation. You search these listings at www.tes.com. If you did not graduate with a degree in education, there are still a ton of options open to you. Look to locations such as South Korea, Mainland China, Japan, Taiwan, or Hong Kong. There are literally TONS of jobs in these countries that will take anyone with a four-year degree (in any discipline) and a passport from an Anglophone country. Locations in the Middle East often pay excellent salaries, but the requirements (education and experience) for these jobs is often more substantial. I spent ten years living and working in South Korea. By the time that I left, I was able to (very easily) save $40,000 per year. At this point in my career, I had several advanced degrees and extensive experience. However, there are still great earning and saving opportunities for recent graduates. Let's take a look at what a recent graduate can earn and save teaching English in South Korea.

Take Home Salary: $2,200

Rent: $0 Apartment is provided by school.

Cost of Airfare: $0 Airfare is paid by school.

Cell Phone: $30

Utilities: $75

Health Insurance: $45 Half of the premiums are covered by the school.

Car: $0 Excellent Public Transport

Public Transport: $50

Groceries: $400

Eating Out / Drinks / Entertainment: $400

As someone who's lived in South Korea, I can say that the figures for groceries and eating out are generous. You are not going to be doing without. You can still go out with friends, meet people, and enjoy your time there. Living in Asia is an amazing experience, and South Korea is one of the most amazing countries in Asia. Your early twenties are a once in a lifetime experience. With this budget, you won't miss out on anything. You can enjoy every minute of your time there. This brings your total monthly expenses to exactly $1,000 per month. This leaves you $1,200 a month to funnel toward your Coast FIRE goals. Let's see how this impacts our Coast FIRE calculations.

We're going to assume the same *$1,500 for monthly expenses, 4% safe withdrawal rate, 6% real rate of return*, and a *target age of 60 for full retirement*.

Full FIRE Number: ($1,500 X 12) = $18,000 / .04 = $450,000

Coast FIRE Number: $450,000 / 1.06 ^ 34 = $62,060

This means that you would need to save $62,060 by age 26. This would allow this sum to grow to $450,000 by age 60.

Let's see how long this would take, assuming a 6% annual rate of return and that you start with no savings.

After four years, you would $64,709! You would have EXCEEDED your Coast FIRE target… and you're only 26! That means that you can stop saving for retirement (assuming that you're going to take advantage of geoarbitrage once you reach full retirement).

The awesome thing that this doesn't account for is that many schools offer severance pay that is equal to one month of pay at the end of your one-year contract. If you resign with that same school, you often receive one-month's salary as a bonus. So, if you complete five contracts, that would be five months of salary that you would also be getting (over $10,000). Also, as an employee in South Korea, you are required to pay into the public pension system. Both you and your employer make contributions each month. At the end of your time in Korea, you may be entitled to a refund for those contributions. It usually amounts to about one month's salary for each year that you work! All totaled, that could mean an extra $20,000 dollars that is coming your way in addition to your regular salary payments – along with a paid plane ticket home.

It's also important to note that these projections don't include overtime – which is often readily available. Some opportunities paying $50 per hour or more!

The thing I love so much about this approach to Coast FIRE is that it doesn't require you to sacrifice all that much. If anything, you get to enjoy MORE experiences than a lot of people your age. In my time in South Korea, I never missed a chance to go out for dinner or drinks, meet people from all around the world, or travel throughout the country (also very cheap). If teaching isn't what you want to do for the rest of your life, that's fine. You're still so young when you get out that you have ample time to pursue the career that you studied for or go back to graduate school. Maybe you'll find that teaching **IS** something you want to pursue. If that's the case, then you'll be well-positioned to earn the income you need to cover your living expenses while taking advantage of geoarbitrage. Now that you've hit your Coast FIRE number, this could be the time to go teach on the beach in Bali or Thailand!

Keep in mind that while these projections are geared toward young people with more time to let their investments grow, people of all ages can choose to live and teach abroad – often with little or no teaching experience. In addition to the ability to save, the lifestyle and experiences make for a terrific return on investment.

PART III
Ready to Hit the Coast

Let me begin by saying that making my home in a low cost of living country has REALLY helped me to achieve Coast FIRE. Many folks back home in America have to work full-time (and more) simply to cover their living expenses. In Europe, the cost of living is much lower. Perhaps most importantly, I don't have the same concerns regarding health insurance that exist in America. I feel that I can live comfortably on 1,000 euros a month. So, before getting to questions and concerns to address before you decide to Coast FIRE, I want to talk about what have been the biggest differences for me.

Benefits of Coast FIRE

Physical Health

This has been one of the biggest benefits for me. I have always made health and fitness a priority in my life. Even with a busy schedule, I made it a point to do some exercise. But it seemed that I was always trying to squeeze in a quick workout before I jumped on the computer. Now, I start my morning with an hour of stretching and yoga. I've been able to set a schedule for running, hiking, swimming, and weight training that has allowed me to feel better than I have in years without overtraining. Without a doubt, the schedule that's now most important to me is my exercise schedule.

With more free time, I also have the opportunity to eat a healthier diet. I used to find myself eating because I had time. I often had five or six classes in a row with ten-minute breaks in between. Instead of sitting down and eating a healthy meal, I would often have a granola bar or some other quick snack. I wasn't eating an unhealthy diet, but I wasn't focusing on doing what was best for my health. Now, fresh fruits, vegetables and lean proteins make up the base of my diet.

__Mental Health__

Before I left my job, I had literally no free time. Normally, that doesn't bother me at work. If I'm engaged in something that I really love, I can happily grind out long hours. The problem was that I wasn't engaged in something I loved. Actually, I hated what I was doing. I used to finish work on Thursday afternoon and sit with my head down for ten minutes just to decompress (my work week was from Sunday to Thursday). I relished my two days off. Even though I had work-related responsibilities, I was able to do them on my own time. Usually Saturday night, my pre-work anxiety would set it – "I can't believe I have to go back to work tomorrow." Eventually it got to the point where I was waking up Friday morning and thinking, "Tomorrow is Saturday, so I'll have to start thinking about going back to work on Sunday." I was either working at a job that I hated, or I was dreading going to work at a job that I hated. Being free of that mindset has literally changed my life. I appreciate everything so much more. Moreover, I have TIME to appreciate everything. I can wake up slowly with my coffee or sit and enjoy a glass of wine at the beach in the evenings. Knowing that I have more control over my schedule has been the best thing about entering into Coast FIRE.

Taking Back Sunday

I can't remember the last time that I had a Sunday off. It has been YEARS! I used to joke that my Sundays were always a minimum of 10-hour days. In addition to the classes that I taught, I did a lot of writing and content creation. It was hard to be always on the go when everyone else is enjoying their day off. Now, I'm more in tune with the world around me. I get up, go to a café for coffee, sometimes go out for breakfast. I slow down and enjoy the day and I appreciate every minute of it.

Another huge advantage of Sundays off is travel planning. Not only was I required to work on Sunday, but Sunday was my busiest day. I used to have to book my travel around my work schedule. If I went away for the weekend, I could stay with friends on Friday night, but I would always need to find a hotel for Saturday night. Oftentimes, I had to request (and pay for) late checkout on Sundays, so I had enough time to finish my work. Freedom from that schedule has saved me both money and aggravation.

Hobbies, Interests, and Side Hustles

Writing is something that I love. I've always loved it. I enjoy blogging, writing books, and creating teaching materials for students all over the world. I even make a few dollars doing it. The amount of money that I make writing doesn't justify me doing it full-time, so my paid employment (which I hated) had to take precedence. Now, I have the time and energy to pursue the things that I love. Earning money toward covering my monthly expenses is a bonus. But the best part is the freedom to do the things that I enjoy the most.

In addition to pursuing things that I've always loved, I now have the time to learn new things and pursue new interests. In an effort to be healthier, I've decided to take up cooking as a hobby. I also have time to devote to learning the language in my new home country. These new hobbies don't have to add to your monthly expenses. There is literally a wealth of free material on YouTube that allows you to learn the basics of any new hobby from speaking Italian to basket weaving.

My first week into Coast FIRE, my advice would have been, "If you're thinking about early retirement, DO IT!" Now that a few months have passed, I would temper that recommendation with a little reason and say, "If you're thinking about early retirement, I would seriously consider it. Just remember that there are huge benefits, as well as some drawbacks."

Drawbacks to Coast FIRE

You Still Have to Work!

Remember that Coast FIRE still means that you need to work enough to cover your daily living expenses. You don't want to touch your investments until you are ready for full retirement. Working a more limited schedule has been nothing short of AMAZING for me. However, I still spend a good chunk of my time working. The plans that I had of waking up, reading, writing, exercising, and going to the beach were interrupted by messages from my boss reminding me that I still had deadlines. I still had WAY more time to do these things, but it wasn't as if I was totally free.

Putting Things Off

The first few weeks with a limited work schedule are fantastic. You can sleep a bit later, spend time with people you love, and prioritize things that you let go by the wayside in the past – in my case this was health and fitness. However, after a few weeks and months, you become very aware of the extra time that you have to fill. In a way, not having the pressure of a job can work against you. You might have plans to fill your newfound free time. However, it gets really easy to put things off because you'll always have time to do it now that you don't work as much. Setting a schedule can really help with this.

Use It or Lose It

The notion that you can always go back to work is something that often encourages people to take the early retirement plunge. Just remember that in the time you've been out of the workforce, the job you do has likely changed. You probably haven't. Even if there haven't been huge changes in the skillset required to do your job, you likely won't be as sharp as when you're working every day. If your part-time work is in the same field – then this is less of a concern. If you're doing something more akin to barista FIRE, then you might need to stay abreast of what's happening in your field if you have a desire of going back to work someday.

This is complicated by the fact that many people choose to use Coast FIRE as an opportunity to do something entirely new or something that they're incredibly passionate about. While that's undoubtedly one of the big advantages of Coast FIRE, it can exacerbate the risk of your current skill set deteriorating.

In light of my own experience, both positive and negative, there are some questions I'd encourage you to ask yourself before you decide to Coast FIRE.

Is Coast FIRE Really for You?

Are my annual expenses realistic?

In my mind, this is the most important question to ask because it's simply the biggest obstacle for most people. And let's face it – it's central to the math that you need to FIRE.

To answer this, ask yourself, "Is my lifestyle going to have to change significantly once I begin to Coast?" Be honest with yourself. One of my close friends purchased a new Volvo not too long ago. It was her dream car (*Really. A Volvo was her dream car. Anyway…*) It was an expensive purchase that required her to make payments each month. Once she paid it off, she was able to channel more money to savings and investments. However, cars don't last forever. When that dream car you have dies, are you going to be comfortable getting something less expensive? Think seriously about how willing you are to accept the accompanying lifestyle changes you may be forced to make.

I've gone over geoarbitrage at length and by now you know that it's an important part of my approach to Coast FIRE. Be sure to seriously consider how this will impact your life. Will my expenses be THAT much lower in another country? Do you like the finer things in life? Almost every place that I've been to offers expat options at expat prices. Are you going to be the guy that a Southeast Asian entrepreneur is banking on to make him rich? There are places that target rich expats. If you're going to live like that, you're not fully taking advantage of geoarbitrage.

If this sounds like I'm condemning people who like the finer things in life, I'm not. What I am insisting on is that you BE HONEST WITH YOURSELF about what you want and how you're going to get it. I have a friend who I speak often with about geoarbitrage. He enjoys spending time in many low cost of living locations (LCOLs), such as Bali. I visited him a few years back at a fancy villa he was staying at in Bali. When I knocked on the door and he called for me to come in, I entered through the front door and into the kitchen. I didn't see him until he called, "Down here!" I looked down, and he was in the swimming pool – in the kitchen. When he and I speak about geoarbitrage, we each come up with wildly different figures for living in Bali. This is no surprise – I've never lived anywhere that had a pool in the kitchen. But the point is, this guy is honest about the lifestyle that he wants for himself. He won't make a move there until he can afford to live the quality of life that desires. If you have a similar appetite for the good life, factor those costs into your Coast FIRE planning.

How long do I really want to work?

Remember that your Coast FIRE number is based on your full FIRE number, your expected rate of return, and the NUMBER OF YEARS UNTIL FULL RETIREMENT. If you're 40 and use 65 as your full-retirement age, you need to be prepared to work for another 25 years. If you don't, the math isn't going to work. Be honest with yourself. Do you really want to work till you're 65? If you feel that your full retirement age is closer to 60, then use that figure in your calculation. You'll have to save more because you'll have fewer years for your portfolio to grow, but you won't be living out your last years of Coast FIRE hating your work and watching the clock.

Can I really live abroad?

How tolerant are you? How patient are you? Do you have a knack for learning languages? Do you expect things to be done "the American way?" Will I miss family and friends? Am I going to go back so much that it doesn't make sense to leave in the first place? All your savings get eaten up by travel. Don't be one of those people that says, "Well, you can always go back!" Yeah, you can. But there's a real cost to that. Moving isn't cheap. Moving overseas is even "more not cheap." If you are not sure if you want to live somewhere, do a six-month trial run. Rent a place in the new country. Put your stuff at home in storage. If you own a home, rent it out. Then, make a decision. This will add to your cost, but you're buying insurance – the insurance to go back to your old life if you feel moving abroad was a mistake.

Who are my friends?

A lot of people overlook this question, and I think it's a huge mistake. Wherever you are on your FIRE path, friendship and socializing are important. If you and your friends enjoy going out to sit at a fancy bar and pay for $15 cocktails, then you're probably still going to do this once you start to Coast too. Remember that you're the one who is making the decision to pursue Coast FIRE – not your friends. If you currently run in a social circle that involves a lot of FIRE or Coast FIRE adherents (or your friends are just frugal), then this may not impact you all that much. Whatever you decide to do, be honest with yourself about your monthly expenses – and how going out with friends is going to affect this.

___Is there a real benefit to Coast FIRE for me?___

So many of the FIRE adherents that I know are highly motivated people. They work hard, they're determined, and they're usually highly skilled and accomplished. If your job is killing you, then you need to get out. Coast FIRE can be a great escape plan. But if your work and your lifestyle aren't problematic, think twice about **_why_** you really want to pursue Coast FIRE. Was it a goal that you set a long time ago? Have things changed in your life? Again, FIRE adherents are often goal oriented. It's easy to get so fixated on a goal that you can't see the forest for the trees. If you hit your Coast FIRE number, that doesn't mean you **_have to_** leave simply because you've set that goal. Be flexible. Think about whether it's still the path you want to pursue or if something in your life has changed. I absolutely love the life I've been able to lead since achieving Coast FIRE, but it isn't for everyone. If you're going to leave behind a life that you really enjoy, make sure that you're going to something better.

Think about the above questions seriously and decide if you're really ready – not just financially, but for the accompanying lifestyle change. Listed below are some things that have really helped me to adjust to life in Coast FIRE.

Suggestions

Save something (even if it's a little)

The whole idea of Coast FIRE is that you've already done the heavy lifting for retirement – now you just coast. You've grown your investments to a point that you can allow the magic of compounding to do the work. You only need to cover your monthly expenses. However, you need to remember that your Coast FIRE number is not a hard and fast guaranteed retirement number. There are still a lot of factors that are outside of your control. Remember, in calculating your Coast FIRE number, you need to think about your withdrawal rate, the return on your investments, and inflation. While you do have control over how much you choose to withdraw in retirement, you have far less control over what markets return and what inflation does. The bottom line – there's still risk involved.

If you're like me, you're risk averse and always concerned about running out of money. Continuing to add to your investments after you've hit Coast FIRE is a great way to mitigate against the effects of market risk and inflationary pressures. You don't necessarily need to be grinding out long hours at work while scraping and saving for every penny - just continue to drop a few dollars a month into your investments. There are advantages to this beyond the additional savings.

It's fun! Investing can be an enjoyable endeavor. If you've reached the point of early retirement, you've likely done it by becoming savvy about where you put your money. Being actively engaged in what's going on with your portfolio can and should be an interest that you have during early retirement.

You can delve into new asset classes. If you're someone who subscribes to modern portfolio theory, then the bulk of your investments are likely composed of a mix of stocks and bonds. If you've already reached your Coast FIRE number, you can begin adding emerging asset classes to your portfolio. You may consider trading cryptocurrency or options. You could also engage in peer-to-peer lending. While these all have the potential for higher returns, they also carry substantial risk. You do have a chance of losing the entirety of your investment.

The mental health benefits are huge.
When I finished college, I was given a book about simple steps to happiness in life. One thing I remember reading was to always save a little bit of money, regardless of how small your salary is. If you can only save $5 a month, then that's what you save. Just save something. It gives you the feeling of continuing to march ahead. It creates a momentum in your life that can extend beyond your finances. If you've worked really hard saving to hit your retirement number, it can feel strange when you stop – even unfulfilling. If you don't believe me, run a projection with your Coast FIRE figure, your expected rate of return, years to full retirement, and a monthly contribution of zero. You should have a figure that equals what you need to survive in full retirement (without working at all). Now run the same projection and add $200 a month to it until you reach full retirement. The difference can be staggering! That small contribution each month can make a huge difference in retirement. Knowing that you're contributing toward that goal also helps you feel productive and fulfilled.

Don't Neglect Your Emergency Fund

If you're like me, you've likely got your investments in a mix of brokerage (after-tax) accounts as well as tax-advantaged retirement accounts (such as an IRA, 401k, SEP, or SIMPLE). Remember, you're not touching these because they are busy enjoying the magical benefits of compounding. However, you may (and almost certainly will) come across unexpected expenses once you decide to Coast FIRE. To meet these unexpected needs, you're going to have to tap into your emergency fund.

It's generally a good idea to set up an emergency before you even start investing for retirement.

The money in your EF should be held in highly liquid assets (cash or cash equivalents), that you can draw on at any time. For simplicity's sake, let's say you keep this in a money market. How much you choose to keep in your emergency fund is dependent on how much comfort and security you feel you need. It is often believed that six months of expenses is a good place to start. Some people choose to have one year. Just remember that there is an opportunity cost to holding cash in your EF. Money market rates are very low – VERY LOW. Interest rates are near zero and there is currently upward pressure on prices.

This means the real value of the money in your EF can actually decrease over time.

It's always a good idea to add a bit to your EF each month. Let's take a look at why.

Suppose you are taking advantage of geoarbitrage and living in a place with a very low cost of living (allowing you to Coast FIRE even earlier than most). *Your monthly expenses are $1,500 USD. Six months of expenses is $9,000. You decide to round up for a little extra security and keep $10,000 in your EF.*

Assuming 2% inflation over ten years, that $10,000 is only going to be worth $7,811.

At 3% inflation, that same $10,000 is only going to have $7440 in buying power.

So, it's a good idea to keep adding to your EF periodically.

Let's assume 2.5% inflation. You would need $12,800 in ten years' time to have roughly the same buying power that you have today with $10,000. That only requires you to add approximately $20 to your EF each month.

I actually prefer to keep a larger emergency fund. For me, geoarbitrage is a huge part of how I am able to pull off Coast FIRE. However, you never know when life may require you to head back to America (or wherever you call home) where things can be much more expensive.

Before you say it… "That'll never happen to me! I'm never going back!" You never know. There are a variety of reasons that you may have to go back. A friend or relative gets sick and needs you? There is a funeral that you need to attend? You need medical care that's unavailable in your country of residence? Or there may be reasons that you WANT to go back. Maybe there's a wedding? A graduation? A reunion? Or maybe you just miss home after all these years? The bottom line is that your emergency fund brings you the comfort, the security, and the flexibility to meet these needs.

If utilizing geoarbitrage is part of your strategy for Coast FIRE, then you may want to consider a slightly larger EF. Even if you hit Coast FIRE with a smaller EF, you can build this out to meet the needs that may arise from emergency travel to your home country. So, you can start out with a smaller emergency fund, and then to continue to grow it over time. This will put you in a better position to absorb those larger expenses.

Don't Neglect Your Emergency Fun

While the importance of an emergency fund can't be overstated – especially for those adhering to Coast FIRE, you shouldn't have to wait for a special occasion to do something you really want to do. While a bit of frugality is also a part of Coast FIRE, you don't want to put yourself in a position where you NEED to deprive yourself of the things that you want. That's where your other EF comes in – your **emergency fun money**.

Coast FIRE is a phenomenal lifestyle and presents terrific opportunities. Just bear in mind that these are only opportunities. They mean nothing if you don't take advantage of them to do the things that you always dreamed to do. I was lucky to find a place where I could live cheaply and enjoy a great lifestyle. The beaches in Portugal are amazing, but there are a lot of other places that are just as amazing. I don't want to have to give up the opportunity to explore them. So, I make sure that I put away some emergency fun money each month. It doesn't have to be a lot. I try to stash away $100 a month for fun expenses. I usually pick low-cost destinations for travel, and my digital nomad lifestyle allows me to save money on long-term accommodation. So, I don't need a ton of extra money above what I have budgeted for my monthly expenses. My emergency fun money covers the cost of my airfare, fuel for road trips, Airbnb's, hostels, or whatever I might want or need for my trip. If I am planning a trip where airfare is going to be more expensive (such as Southeast Asia), I try to add a few extra bucks to this EF each month before I go. Bear in mind that destinations like Southeast Asia often have far lower daily living costs. In Indonesia, I can rent both a motorbike and a studio apartment for $200 a month. Eating (well) only costs me about $10 a day. Therefore, the more substantial cost of travel to these destinations is offset by the lower cost of living throughout your time there. I might need $1,000 to fly to Bali, but I can live there for less than $1,000 a month. That's a $500 savings on my monthly expenses. If I stay for two months, what I save in living costs pays for my ticket. The point being, you don't need to save a ton into this second EF, but it's a great way to ensure that you always have a little extra to do all the things that you always wanted. It doesn't necessarily have to be travel. I have a friend who loves wine. He budgets a little extra each month to make sure that he and his significant other can enjoy a wine tasting with gourmet food. Just make sure you are not depriving yourself of anything while you're coasting toward FI. Which brings me to my next bit of advice…

Make It Happen

When you first decide to pull the plug on full-time work, you might be totally burnt out and just in need of some serious downtime. This was definitely the case for me. The thing is, once your batteries are recharged, you're going to need to focus that energy somewhere. Since you don't have a full-time job to devote yourself to, you need to have other interests. Whatever it is you plan to do in early retirement, make it happen. Maybe right now, you just want to sit around and read every book on your shelf that you always said you'd read if you had time. Or maybe you just want to binge watch Netflix. Whatever you do to veg out and relax, this can only last for so long – trust me!

Now is the chance to do the things that you always said you were going to do. If you are working remotely, take the opportunity to travel and live as a digital nomad. If you're tied to your current location because you still need to physically go into the office, then pursue the dreams and interests that you had been planning to. Don't sit at home and lounge around while you put in your part-time schedule. If I were doing that, I would just prefer to continue working my full-time job and bring myself closer to my full FI number. You've given yourself the gift of time – don't waste it!

Be Accountable

In order to make things you always dreamed of a reality, you need to clearly identify the things that you want to do. What are your goals? I'm a big believer in writing things down. Create a list of what you want to accomplish. Start with a long-term goal and break it down into monthly, weekly, and daily milestones. Even more important than writing your goals down, share your goals with others. There are tons of groups on *Facebook* where people share common interests. You can also get involved in groups through the *Meet Up* app. When you share your goals with like-minded people, they're more likely to hold you accountable for what you need to do to achieve them. Remember, this is **your** time. There's no boss looking over your shoulder. It's incredibly easy to put things off. Make sure you're still marching in the direction of your goals.

Set a Schedule

Part of holding yourself accountable is setting a schedule. I know you might be thinking, "Wait a minute! I just got out of a job where I had a strict work schedule. I want to take it easy!" Again, that's fine for the first month or so, but eventually you need to get moving. I set a schedule for writing because that's what I love to do. A lot of people consider writing to be work, but I don't. Nonetheless, I need to prioritize my time so that I can accomplish all the things that I want to. Your schedule doesn't have to include things that you consider to be work, and it doesn't even need to be full-time. For example, you might plan to do a hike every Tuesday and Friday morning at 9 am. I make sure that I stretch for an hour every morning at 6 am. It's a small thing, but making it part of my daily schedule helps me to be sure that I incorporate it into my routine every day. Another reason that having a schedule is so important to me is that my work is done asynchronously. I can easily finish my work in a day or a day and a half. I could just as easily spread that work out over five days with an hour here or there. I prefer to get all my work done for my employer on Mondays and Tuesdays. Then, I can have the rest of the week to be fully devoted to my own personal goals. Finally, a schedule means nothing if you don't stick to it. Make sure you stick to it! If you planned to do something at 9 am, then don't start at 9:15 because you got *a late start on the day*. You wouldn't have shown up late to your full-time job. Being prompt is as important in your pursuit of your own goals is it is in your pursuit of someone else's.

Do Some Professional Development

So, what exactly should your schedule consist of? One thing that I feel strongly about is continuing to develop yourself and your skills while you're coasting toward full retirement. This may be something to keep your skills up to date in your current field (if that's how you're covering your monthly expenses), or it may be something in your new field. For example, maybe you've moved to a low-cost of living country to teach English while taking advantage of geoarbitrage. You could choose to take some online classes in education or even do a TEFL certificate. Maybe your Coast FIRE plans involve pursuing a university qualification in an entirely new field. That's great, but your professional development doesn't have to be something expensive or time consuming. Just keep moving forward. It's another way of adding flexibility and a layer of security to your FI journey. You never know if and when you may want to go back into the workforce full-time. Keeping your mind and your skills sharp is never a bad thing.

NOTE: Many foreign universities offer excellent education at a fraction of the price of US universities.

Build That Passive Income

Coast FIRE gives us the time to do what we love – and that should be the first priority. If you get stuck into constantly trying to make money, it really defeats the purpose of reaching financial independence. Having said that, finding a way to monetize one of your hobbies to build passive income is a good idea for Coast FIRE adherents. It can be a huge boost to your finances – both now and in the future. Since you're still working to cover your monthly expenses, any passive income that you begin to produce from a hobby or side hustle can reduce the number of hours you need to work to meet your monthly expenses. Since you're likely going to rely on your investments when you reach full-retirement age, adding another passive income stream (or two) can give you a more secure and diversified financial approach when you do reach full retirement. Even if it's part-time and brings in a few hundred bucks, plant the seed and water with the extra time that you have. Who knows? It might even wind up replacing your need to work all together!

Ideas for Passive Income

*There are literally countless ideas for side hustles, but not all are passive. Since you are already working to cover your monthly expenses, this list is composed of activities that you can enjoy doing and still earn a bit of cash on the side.

- *Blogging*

Building a successful blog is a lot of hard work. However, if you are writing about something that you enjoy, it may feel a lot less like work. There are tons of easy and affordable website builders and hosting plans that make blogging accessible to anyone regardless of technical knowledge or ability. Most bloggers make their money through affiliate income, though some earn income through advertising revenue.

- *A YouTube Channel*

You could probably figure out how to do almost anything on Earth by watching a free video available on YouTube. Whatever your interest or hobby, you may wish to share your knowledge of this on YouTube. YouTubers often earn revenue from affiliates and advertising. Now, YouTube has developed a paid membership subscription, thereby offering another avenue to earn revenue through your digital content.

- ***Shopify / Etsy***

If you want to build out your own online store and do your own marketing, you may choose to sell on Shopify. Etsy is another online sales platform that allows customers to search for your product on their platform. You have to do less marketing with Etsy. You have to pay to set up your store on Shopify, whereas Etsy is free to join (but they do take a cut of what you make).

- ***Teachers Pay Teachers***

If you are a teacher that is heading toward early retirement, you might choose to capitalize on all those old lesson plans that you've written over the years. There is a free membership and a premium membership ($60 per year). The premium membership allows you to keep a larger percentage of your sales. Some teachers have done so well on this platform that they've retired from teaching to do TpT full-time.

- ***Online Courses***

If you have specialized knowledge that is in demand, you can turn it into an online course. Once you've completed the course, students pay for the video content and online tutorials that you've created. You don't need to actually teach anything, so the income is passive. There are a variety of platforms that can host your online course. Some (*Udemy*) are free to join. Others (*Thinkific* or *Coursera*) offer more functionality, but require a membership fee. *Udemy does* take a large cut of your sales if students find your course on their platform.

- ***Online Books***

If you enjoy writing (like me), you can choose to create E-books on anything under the sun. Some people love writing fiction, others write how-to books – the possibilities are limitless. *Amazon Kindle Direct Publishing* (*KDP*) offers a very generous percentage of sales to authors, provided that you opt in to their *KDP Select* program. By choosing this option, you agree to sell your book only on *Amazon*. Another advantage of selling on *Amazon* is that they will print and ship individual paperbacks of your title if readers don't have a *Kindle*. If you choose not to sell on *Amazon* (or not to opt into *KDP Select*), you can explore other platforms. *Payhip* is free and easy to set up. It also allows authors to keep 95% of their sales. However, the traffic is nothing compared to *Amazon*. You can also choose to sell your E-book through your blog (if it has e-commerce functionality) or use your blog to link to your *Amazon* or *Payhip* listing.

- ***Selling Your Art / Photography***

If painting, drawing, or taking photos is something you enjoy, you might be able to capitalize on what you love. I have a friend who is a full-time RVer. She is also a talented painter. She offers her paintings to display in local bars, cafes, and lounges. Since the quality of her work is outstanding, these business owners are often happy to have the free and beautiful décor. There is a small tag placed in the corner indicating that the work is for sale. When a customer makes a purchase, she gives the owner of the establishment a cut of the sales price. It's a win – win!

The rest of the items on this list require a minimal amount of effort & I still consider them to be passive.

- **Recruiting**

Many companies will pay a finder's fee for talented employees. See if any exist in your field of expertise. I worked in education for fifteen years. Many schools will pay anywhere from $25 to $200 for successful teacher candidates. Often this involves sharing a link that identifies you as the person referring them to the company (a referral link) and extolling the benefits of working for that company. You may get peppered with questions from potential candidates. This is one of the downsides. You need to make the decision as to how much of your own valuable time you're willing to share (particularly if that candidate is unlikely to be successful).

- **House Hacking**

Rental real estate is a terrific way to build passive income. However, with rental properties come additional monthly payments (taxes, insurance, and homeowner's association fees) – not to mention the headache associated with doing repairs. For your own home, you have to do these things anyway. If you already own your own home, you can simply rent it out on Airbnb or VRBO as a short-term rental. I know a lot of people may be hesitant to have a roommate – even if it does mean extra income. I completely understand because I am one of those people. However, if you're going to travel, there's nothing wrong with offsetting the cost of your trip by renting your primary residence during the time that you're away. Check on the local regulations in your town / city and any restrictions imposed by your homeowner's association (if you have one). Similarly, you may be able to rent out your car, your bicycle(s), or other items around the house. I have a friend who rents his beach house on Airbnb. He includes his surfboard for 20 euros extra per day. Not a bad way to increase the return on your vacation rental!

Give Back in Some Way

This isn't a side hustle or a money maker, but it definitely is something that will enrich your life. For most people, their work is a big part of what gives their life meaning. One of the biggest hurdles that I dealt with when I transitioned to Coast FIRE was that I wasn't doing anything meaningful. That's actually a big part of why I left my full-time job earlier than I anticipated. The first month or two was great! I enjoyed spreading my work out over time and not being rushed to meet deadlines. But eventually, I felt like I needed to do more. Find some time to do something to help others. It could be an hour a week or even an hour a month. I find it's 100% necessary for navigating the psychological hurdles associated with moving from being a workaholic to feeling like you have all the time in the world.

If you're still in the USA, you can check *VolunteerMatch*, the *United Way*, or even your local *YMCA*. If you're abroad, you can check out *International Voluntary Service*. Just a note of caution. There are a lot of 'volunteer' programs that charge participants in an effort to 'cover the expenses' associated with your placement. I know some people who've had great experiences with these programs, but I choose to avoid them. In no way am I saying that you should avoid them too – just be aware that they exist if and when you choose to do volunteer work.

PART IV
Life on the Coast

When do I start tapping my investments?

If you've managed to accumulate substantial savings and investments, that's great! Just remember, that ***you're not going to touch these investments until your FULL retirement age***. These investments are to be left so that they can grow via the magic of compound returns. The money that you need to cover your expenses in Coast FIRE needs to come from your income. This is money that you earn through work, your business, or a side hustle of some sort. This is not investment income – that cash needs to be reinvested. For example, if you've got $100,000 in dividend stocks that pay you 4%, that $4,000 per year should NOT go towards your living costs. It needs to be reinvested to buy new shares of stock.

What about when I hit full-retirement age?

Once you hit retirement, you are going to want to assess your tax situation and see how your investment account withdrawals will impact the tax you owe. You also need to consider your full-retirement age and how that impacts the tax consequences of your withdrawals. Many tax-advantaged retirement accounts (such as a traditional

IRA, SEP IRA, or a Keogh account) have a minimum age of 59 and a half before you can begin taking distributions. If your full-retirement age is earlier than 59 and a half, then you can't access these accounts for daily living expenses without paying an early withdrawal penalty of 10%. If you have a Roth IRA, you can always take tax-free distributions of your contributions at any time (that's because contributions to a Roth are made with after-tax money). However, if you dip into the earnings on your Roth before 59 and a half, you will encounter a penalty.

If you have a taxable brokerage account, then this may be the easiest source of income to tap. Many online brokers, like Schwab and Fidelity, have online dashboards that are incredibly easy to navigate. If you have a security that pays a dividend or interest each year, there is usually a question that asks you if you want to reinvest those distributions. Next to that question, there is usually a box that you tick to have those funds reinvested. While you are working toward Coast FIRE, and even after you achieve Coast FIRE, these boxes should all be ticked – so that all distributions are being reinvested. This is helping your nest egg to grow. But now you are no longer working and need this income to cover your daily living expenses. It's as easy as going into your account and unticking those boxes. This will deposit those distributions to your brokerage account as a cash balance. You can then make an online transfer from your brokerage account to the bank account that is linked to your online broker. This is not requiring you to actually sell any shares of your securities. You are simply picking the fruit off the tree – not chopping the tree down.

What should I use to cover my living expenses and in what order?

Before 59 and a half you may incur a penalty on certain tax-advantaged retirement accounts. Consider sourcing income from the following investments (and in the following order) once you hit your full FIRE number.

#1 – Passive Income from business or side hustles (book royalties, advertising income, or online sales)

#2 – Distributions (interest & dividends) from your taxable brokerage account as described above

#3 – Selling shares in your brokerage account or taking contributions from your Roth IRA.

This is specific to your tax situation and your living costs. If your living costs are low, you will likely have a smaller total taxable income (and perhaps no tax liability). If this is the case, it would likely make sense to sell shares in your taxable brokerage. This will likely trigger a taxable event that you will owe capital gains taxes on. The amount you owe will depend on your total income and how long you've held that security. At the time of writing, if you have a low taxable income (less than $40,000) and the sale of the shares is considered a long-term capital gain, you will owe no tax.

After age 59 and a half, you can begin to tap your other investment accounts without the 10% early withdrawal penalty. Also consider when you want to take Social Security and how that will offset your expenses in retirement.

When should I take Social Security?

At the time of writing, you will be eligible for early retirement at age 62. However, the longer you delay your retirement, the larger your benefit will be. Many people ask me when the best time is to take Social Security. Without knowing how long you're going to live, it's an impossible question to answer. I tell those people to consider their needs at the time. If you desperately need that additional income to cover your expenses in retirement, then it makes sense to take it earlier. If the passive income from your side hustles, along with distributions from your investment accounts is easily covering your living expenses, you might choose to wait. It is also important to consider market conditions at the time. If delaying social security requires you to take a large chunk of your investments during a down market, you may be exposing yourself to sequence-of-returns risk. If the market is performing well, you may wish to tap into your investments and wait for that larger social security check. It is often difficult to beat the guaranteed increase in monthly income that comes with delaying Social Security. Finally, if you're in poor health, you may wish to consider taking retirement benefits earlier.

Part of making an informed decision about Social Security benefits is to continue to monitor what your future benefit payment will be. The Social Security website (ssa.gov) makes this incredibly easy. It tracks your earnings history. Make sure that the information on the website accurately reflects your earnings history. Another great tool that the website has is it lets you see how much your payment will increase by delaying it each year. You can run different projections for different ages.

How do I approach rebalancing?

You should be revisiting your portfolio at least once a year to ensure that you maintain your target allocation. However, once you get closer to full-retirement age, you may need to readjust your target allocation. Just as your original allocation should reflect your appetite for risk, as you move closer to your full retirement age, you should become more risk averse. This means adjusting your allocation so that a larger portion of your investments are in bonds as opposed to stocks. While equities offer a larger potential return, they tend to be more volatile. Accepting the lower returns that bond funds offer will leave you less exposed to the potential larger downturns in the market. Historically, even when the stock market declines sharply, it regains its value. However, this takes time – sometimes years. You don't always have the luxury of time in retirement – when you will be depending on these investments to cover your living expenses. Establish and update your investment allocation based on a level of risk that you feel comfortable with. It's always a good idea to seek out a financial professional to assist you with this.

Tax and Residency Concerns

If part of your Coast FIRE strategy involves going abroad to take advantage of geoarbitrage, it's a good idea to consider the tax implications of your move abroad. When I listed potential locations abroad in Part II, I mentioned that some countries have especially high tax rates. Portugal offers ten years of tax-advantages residency through a program called Non-Habitual Residency. However, after this expires, you start to pay taxes as any resident would – and they're high. The good news is that after five years you can get a passport, which brings you all the benefits of EU citizenship, and not be a tax resident. Just ensure that you spend more than 183 days outside the country (think six months and a day in Southeast Asia). Both Portugal and Spain have wealth taxes on their residents, and the threshold is quite low – 600,000 and 700,000 euros, respectively. Not all asset types are included in this figure, so speak to a local accountant to find out what if any obligation you might have for this tax. Once you Coast FIRE, you want to keep your expenses as low as possible (so you have to work as little as possible). Ensure that you limit the amount of income that gets eaten up by tax.

Ties to America

If you're an American planning to move abroad, or you've already made the move, it's a good idea to keep an address and state residency in the USA. If you work with an accountant in the USA, they may let you use their address to receive official documents or financial statements. Another simple option is to use a mail forwarding service. Popular options include *Traveling Mailbox, Post Scan Mail, Earth Class Mail,* or *Virtual Post*. I currently use *Post Scan Mail* and have been satisfied with their service. You may decide to simply use a relative's home or a mail forwarding service in the state you've most recently called home. This is fine and often the most convenient option. Just be aware of the potential state tax implications of the state you choose to call home. Even if you claim the foreign earned income exclusion, this only excludes **earned** income. It doesn't exclude other types of investment income. Since America is one of only two countries in the world that has citizenship-based taxation, you may be unnecessarily adding to your tax bill by choosing to make your home in a state with a high state income tax.

A simple and popular option is to make South Dakota your home state. The state of

South Dakota has no state income tax. In order to establish residency, you simply need to spend one night at a hotel in the state. You can then set up a mail forwarding service account (in South Dakota). You're able to then get a SD driver license and be an official state resident. You're also able to register to vote in South Dakota. There are many advantages to this. First and foremost, it gives you a home base in the USA to receive any important documents that you may need. Those can be scanned and, if necessary, forwarded to you abroad. You're able to open a bank account in South Dakota with this type of residency, something that you may have difficulty doing in other states without a home address. Similarly, applying for credit cards in the USA requires a US address. The address that is linked to your credit card is also important. When ordering online with a US credit card, you are usually asked for your billing address (or at least the zip code). Many sites (not all, but many) will reject US cards that have foreign billing addresses. Federal issues that require state residency are less convoluted. For example, when Covid-19 hit and I wanted to be vaccinated, it was difficult to establish which state I was able to get my vaccine in – because I wasn't a legal resident of any US state. Having state residency makes life a lot easier.

US Phone Number

Part of staying on top of your finances involves checking on your accounts regularly. Many financial institutions require a one-time passcode (OTP) to access your account. This is an important security measure that helps keep your account safe. However, it can be problematic when living abroad. This should not be an issue in today's globalized society, but many huge banks have software that won't accept phone numbers that don't conform to the standard US format. That is, a three-digit area code, three-digit exchange, followed by four additional numbers. Again this shouldn't be a problem, but it has been for me. I do my banking in America with two separate banks. One of my banks made my transition abroad seamless. The other has been an absolute nightmare to deal with. One solution for receiving OTPs is to use a Skype number. This is incredibly affordable and also a great option if you frequently call phone numbers back in the USA. The phone number costs about $5 per month if billed annually and you're able to get two-way SMS and unlimited calling to US numbers for $3 per month. It's important to note that even this option doesn't work with all financial institutions. One of my credit card companies was unable to use my Skype number for the necessary OTP. Another possible option among expats is to use Google Fi. Before you go abroad, it's definitely a good idea to check with the financial institutions that will require an OTP for you to access your accounts. Try to establish a solution before you go that will ensure you always have easy access to your accounts while abroad.

Questions to Ask While You Coast

Now that you've officially decided to Coast FIRE, you should continue to reassess the decision that you made. Remember – nothing is forever. Just as we rebalance our portfolio every year, we need to rebalance our mind and ensure the decisions we've made are the ones that have made us happiest. If that's not the case, then make a change.

Am I fulfilled?

Very similar to what you asked yourself before you decided to Coast. Once you pull the trigger, you may find out that you miss work. If you've changed jobs, the work you do may seem less fulfilling to you. All the things that you planned to do with all your free time may not have turned out the way you planned. That new mountain bike is gathering dust in the garage, the language you planned to learn is way too tough, and your desire to learn guitar has resulted in several noise complaints from the neighbors. For some people, Coast FIRE represents a major lifestyle change – one that they may be unprepared for. Some people simply need work. Just because you can afford to do something, doesn't mean that you should. If your best life is in the office, go back and get it.

Do I really wanna work at all?

The questions above all center on whether Coast FIRE is an affordable and realistic option, and whether it's something you want to pursue at all. But, what if Coast FIRE is financially feasible for you? What if living abroad is everything you dreamed it would be? What if you don't miss your old job one bit? What if you love the freedom and flexibility of Coast FIRE so much that you ask yourself, "Why would I ever want to work again – at all?"

Unfortunately, Coast FIRE doesn't work unless you do – at least enough to cover your monthly expenses. For a lot of people the initial relief in their work schedule is a much-welcomed reprieve. But even a limited schedule may be something that you come to dread. As I mentioned earlier, a lot of people equate Coast FIRE with full FIRE – which it's not. I can't count the number of times that I've thought about how nice it would be to be fully retired. That's why the suggestions that I outlined in Part III are so important. These, and a few other strategies, may help you transition to full FIRE faster than you originally planned.

Strategies to Transition to Full FIRE Ahead of Schedule

Keep Investing!!!

This is such an important part of my life in Coast FIRE. I get criticized for it all the time in FIRE circles because people say it's not "true Coast." With respect – screw them. To me the financial independence movement is all about freedom and security. Anything that continues to increase both of those things in my life is super important to me and something I'll always pursue. Again, you don't need to be investing as much as you were when you were working – and you probably won't be. Just keep adding a little bit each month. If you've got your portfolio in a mix of low-cost ETFs, that's great. One thing I continue to look for and invest in is income-producing mutual funds or ETFs. You may also look for individual stocks that pay a nice dividend. Just remember – with individual stocks you are exposing yourself to more risk than you are with funds and ETFs. Having said that, there are a lot of individual stocks out there that can pay a nice dividend above what you may be able to get on a fund or ETF. Keep in mind the correlation between risk and return. Even if you don't build enough to totally stop working, the additional passive income that you generate can reduce the number of hours that you need to work to cover your expenses. If you do begin to build a portfolio of dividend stocks, I would keep it separate from your Coast FIRE portfolio. This will make rebalancing that Coast FIRE portfolio easier each year.

Rentals

Rentals are a phenomenal way to generate passive income. Having said that, this is my least preferred item on this list. So, I'm going to go into a bit of detail on why I think rentals just don't make sense for people who have already started to Coast. Rentals – especially in the USA – have a lot of monthly expenses attached to them. You'll have to pay property taxes, homeowner's insurance, as well as maintenance and repairs on the property. You very well may be responsible for homeowner's association or condo fees. If it's not a condo, add in the cost of lawncare and flood insurance. You're responsible for these things whether your property is occupied or not. If the property is unoccupied, you will probably still need to pay minimal expenses for electricity and water. I've had properties in the southern part of the USA, and I couldn't leave them unoccupied without the air conditioning running. If I did, I would have run into mold problems, which can be both difficult and expensive to get rid of. Expenses add up! Do you need to replace the HVAC? I paid $6,000 to replace one in one of my homes. Do you need new carpeting? In a small rental property, it set me back about $4,000. These figures are actually fairly reasonable. You may find yourself paying significantly more for these types of repairs. God forbid you need to replace the roof! You're probably looking at close to $10,000. Painting isn't cheap either.

All of these things **add** to your monthly expenses. Hopefully, the rents that you're receiving cover these expenses and provide you with additional income to cover **your** monthly expenses. However, this assumes that you do not have to cover a mortgage payment. If you don't have the cash to pay for the house upfront, you'll need to pay the bank for that mortgage each month. This can significantly eat up any income that you had planned on using to cover your monthly living expenses. Yes, it's true that mortgage rates are currently very low, and a significant portion of your mortgage payment will probably go toward the principal balance (building the equity you have in the home). Just remember, you're aiming for positive cash flows right now – not in the future. Having your tenants pay off your mortgage isn't a bad idea, but this is a long game. If you're looking for immediate relief from your monthly expenses in Coast FIRE, this doesn't necessarily provide it. You also need to assume a lot of risk in that you will have to pay those monthly expenses even if the property is not generating rental income. Another concern that I have is the uncertain situation that Covid-19 has created. If the government were to enact protections for renters that prevented evictions, you would essentially be paying for someone else to live in your home – and have no lawful recourse to remove them. So, you can see why I am opposed to adding rental properties to your Coast FIRE portfolio. Having said that, they can produce income.

If you do pursue this path, there are a few things to keep in mind.

If I were to add rental real estate to my Coast FIRE portfolio, I would ensure that I had a larger emergency fund that was set aside specifically for the home(s) that you'll be renting. This would need to be large enough that in the event of one of the unforeseen expenses above, I wouldn't be forced to abandon the lifestyle I enjoy in Coast FIRE.

Play the averages. If the cost of a new roof for your house is $8,000 and it is expected to last for 20 years, then divide the total cost by 240 months and add that to your monthly expenses ($33 per month). If you know you have to replace your HVAC every 15 years and it costs $6,000, then add that average cost to your monthly expenses (another $33 per month). Do this for all your recurring expenses (painting, carpeting, appliances, etc.) and set that amount aside into your rental property emergency fund each month. This will help keep you from being caught off-guard when these expenses rise – and they will arise.

Lower your guaranteed monthly expenses. Repairs and maintenance are unavoidable. However, you can reduce, or avoid altogether, some of your fixed monthly expenses. Don't buy a condo. Condo fees can be outrageous. Further, if the association is not financially sound, you may run into a lot of special assessments. Avoid condos. Similarly, avoid homeowner's associations. I am not anti HOAs. They have a lot of benefits. I think they help to keep neighborhoods looking good and make sure everyone keeps their house looking as they should. Many have amenities like a pool or community center. This is great for your primary residence, but makes little sense for a rental property. Why would you pay for this for someone else? It is true that this often makes the home more desirable for prospective tenants, but is it worth adding those additional expenses each month? Another downside is that some HOAs are very strict. This can add to your maintenance expenses. Finally, choose a location with lower property taxes. This can be a huge monthly savings! Also, the lower cost of living in these areas often means that you can save when you need repairs or maintenance. Remember the person who is repairing your home is making money to pay their own bills.

Build That Side Hustle into a Business

This is easier said than done. I'm a big believer that one of the things you do during Coast FIRE should bring you some income. However, if you want to stop working all together, this needs to be more than a side hustle. And it needs to bring you more than "some income." It needs to cover your monthly expenses – hopefully more. Remember that businesses have down months and even down years. This needs to pay the bills, so you need to treat it like a job – not a hobby. I know people that have poured money into failing businesses. I would personally limit my investment to reinvesting the income that the side hustle is producing. If it's not producing any income, then it's probably not a side hustle that you want to try to turn into a business. You may enjoy what you're doing enough to treat it as a side gig, but ask yourself if you love it enough to devote the time necessary to build a business. If it becomes something you dread doing more than your previous job, you might as well go back to work. If you're looking for ideas for a side business, revisit the ideas I covered in Part II.

Going Back

I cringe as I type. I have no desire to go back to the grind – NONE. AT. ALL. Having said that, there are some people for whom it may make sense. This is particularly true if you're younger and your path to full retirement is a longer one. If Coast FIRE requires you to work for another 20 or 25 years (even if it is part-time) that may be too much for you. Do the math. What would you earn going back to work? What would you be able to save? Most importantly – How long would you have to work in that full-time position to reach full FIRE? If you can reach your full FIRE number with five more years of work, then that might be preferable to working for another 25 years. Again – do the math. Make sure the numbers add up and if it requires a move back to the USA, be sure to add that to your total cost. This book has equipped you with the financial formulas to make informed decisions about your own personal and financial future – that's empowering.

Final Thoughts

First of all, thank you so much for taking the time to purchase and read this book. As an FI-minded individual, I can only assume that you're careful with how you spend your money. I appreciate that you chose to spend some of it on something I wrote. Similarly, I hope that the material in this book was of value to you wherever you are on your journey to Coast FIRE. I mentioned in this book that part of how I approach FIRE may not be consistent with some more traditional aspects of Coast FIRE, but I do what brings me the greatest freedom, comfort, and security. I hope you feel empowered enough to do the same. The ideas in this book are only that – ideas. How you massage them to meet your unique goals is up to you.

As I mentioned so many times, my current lifestyle would never have been possible without geoarbitrage. If you're a person who hasn't explored all the world has to offer outside of your home country, I encourage you to do so. It may not be for you, but you just might be surprised. I know more than a few people who have expressed strong doubts about living abroad, and now these same people can't ever imagine living back home in America ever again. Finally, it's only money. At the end of the day, it's nothing more than a means to achieving the life we want to live. It's not an end in and of itself. I hope your time in Coast FIRE is everything you dreamed it would be. I also hope you enjoy the road you travel on the way there. I love waking up and being able to write most days. But I also look back at my career, and in large part I loved what I did. I think about the times when I was working 14 or 15-hour days, and a lot of that was fun. Towards the end, it was time for me to go, but overall I loved every bit of what I did. Whichever path you choose, remember that you only go around once in this world, so enjoy the ride.

Also by James J. Riley, EdS

Move to Portugal: How I immigrated to Portugal, and how you can too!

Teaching English Online: Leave Home, Live Rich, Retire Early- A How-To Guide for Digital Nomads

Think Success: Fifteen Rules for Establishing and Maintaining a Successful Mindset

Author Bio

James "Jay" Riley is originally from Long Island, New York. He has been an educator for over fifteen years and a world traveler, investor, and entrepreneur his entire life. He holds MBA, MAcc, MA TESOL, and EdS degrees. He has lived, worked, and traveled all over the world, but currently resides in Consolação, Portugal.

www.ingramcontent.com/pod-product-compliance
Lightning Source LLC
Chambersburg PA
CBHW071508220526
45472CB00003B/954